Additional Praise for *Mindfulness*

"Caryn Wells writes with the refreshing and authentic voice of experience—including a year in which she ran two 1,500-student high schools in Michigan. She acknowledges a sad truth about school leadership today: it is not a crisis of shortage, but a lack of leaders who are equipped to deal with the stressors that are an inevitable part of leading. Far from succumbing to the difficulties of that challenge, Wells shares a hopeful plan of action that every school leader can and should embrace." —**Joan Richardson**, editor-in-chief, *Phi Delta Kappan*

"Finding calm in the middle of a storm most appropriately describes the purpose of this well written treatise on the practice of mindfulness: 'to be fully present . . . in the moment . . . to enter into stillness and calm by mindful moments or meditation.' Through self-assessment, examples, and practice, this book provides guidelines to reduce stress and help leaders thrive in the workplace. Pause, take a breath, and take the time to read this book meant for all leaders, especially school leaders." —**Dr. Rosemary Papa**, Del and Jewell Lewis Endowed Chair and professor of educational leadership, Northern Arizona University

"This book explores the path for learning about, understanding, challenging, and thinking about oneself. Dr. Wells introduces the reader to mindfulness and then explores the pathways that lead to a balance in one's life as an educational leader. 'That way of being can contribute to an approach that has a different kind of power, the power that supports, influences, and builds capacity in others.'" —**James Berry**, executive director, National Council of Professors of Educational Administration, and professor of educational leadership, Eastern Michigan University

Mindfulness

How School Leaders Can Reduce Stress and Thrive on the Job

Caryn M. Wells

ROWMAN & LITTLEFIELD
Lanham • Boulder • New York • London

Published by Rowman & Littlefield
A wholly owned subsidiary of The Rowman & Littlefield Publishing Group, Inc.
4501 Forbes Boulevard, Suite 200, Lanham, Maryland 20706
www.rowman.com

Unit A, Whitacre Mews, 26-34 Stannary Street, London SE11 4AB

British Library Cataloguing in Publication Information Available

Library of Congress Cataloging-in-Publication Data
Names: Wells, Caryn M.
Title: Mindfulness : how school leaders can reduce stress and thrive on the job /
    by Caryn M. Wells.
Description: Lanham : Rowman & Littlefield, [2015] | Includes bibliographical references
    and index.
Identifiers: LCCN 2015044130 (print) | LCCN 2016002380 (ebook) |
    ISBN 9781475826203 (cloth : alk. paper) | ISBN 9781475826210 (pbk. : alk. paper) |
    ISBN 9781475826227 (Electronic)
Subjects: LCSH: Educational leadership—Psychological aspects. |
    School administrators—Job stress. | School principals—Job stress. | Mindfulness-based
    cognitive therapy. | Stress management.
Classification: LCC LB2806 .W424 2016 (print) | LCC LB2806 (ebook) |
    DDC 371.2—dc23
LC record available at http://lccn.loc.gov/2015044130

For the three men in my life,
Eric, Elliott, and Brendan

And for the educational leaders who work tirelessly to make a difference in the lives of the students they serve-you have my deepest respect

Contents

A Guide for Reading This Book

This book takes you on a journey of self-discovery, into a world that is often not experienced during the course of leading—it is the place of stillness and quiet, one that offers insights while being in touch with sensing and feeling. It is a world possible through the practice of *mindfulness*. Before you begin reading this book, take a few moments to take the first survey on the next page. Take it again when you finish the book and see where your self-discovery has taken you.

Writing this book was a mindful exercise, one in which I had to push the "pause" button numerous times to slow the process down and practice being in the moment myself. I insert some *mindful pauses* along the way to demonstrate that the intention to be mindful is one that was nurtured when I reminded myself to slow the world down and just *be with* what was happening. I hope that the practices and examples in this book will bring to you, the reader, a chance to slow down your busy world and experience the stillness and the insights available from being in the moment.

There are many practices and samples at the end of the book. They are meant to be copied and taken multiple times to see where you are at any given time; people evolve and times change, so the practices and charts are meant for multiple use. Have fun on your self-discovery—there are some smiles embedded in this text, knowing the amazing power of laughter and ease, something that might not always feel present in the life of a busy school leader.

Survey—Before Starting the Book

You will have an opportunity to complete the same survey at the end of the book.

Directions: Answer each statement to the extent with which you agree or disagree with each.

Key   1. Strongly Disagree   2. Disagree   3. Agree   4. Strongly Agree

		1	2	3	4
1.	I am sure of what to do to manage the stress from work	1	2	3	4
2.	I know how to practice self-compassion	1	2	3	4
3.	I take some time out for mindful moments throughout the day at work	1	2	3	4
4.	I feel patient with things that unfold during the day at work	1	2	3	4
5.	I practice self-care efforts like mindfulness	1	2	3	4
6.	I tend to criticize myself when I make a mistake	1	2	3	4
7.	I tend to deny, project, or blame when I feel attacked by criticism	1	2	3	4
8.	I recognize messages, or "wake-up calls" as they happen at work	1	2	3	4
9.	I feel compassion for people in my school or school district	1	2	3	4
10.	I find it difficult to concentrate and be fully in the present moment at work	1	2	3	4
11.	I sometimes find it hard to empathize with situations I encounter at school or the school district	1	2	3	4
12.	I notice that I don't always listen to what is happening at school or in the school district because I am overwhelmed, distracted, or preoccupied	1	2	3	4
13.	I find moments of stillness during the workday	1	2	3	4
14.	I worry about my ever-growing "to-do" list	1	2	3	4
15.	I spend some time worrying about or regretting things I have done or left undone at work	1	2	3	4

Preface

For my initial two years of medical school, I had sat in lecture halls absorbing a wealth of information about anatomy, physiology, pharmacology, and pathology. During the last two years, I had stood rapt at the bedside, taking in the words of master clinicians who revealed the subtleties of physical examination and the fine points of medical treatment. Brimming with new knowledge, I thought I was fully ready to assume the care of people. I mistook information for insight. While I was well prepared for the science, I was pitifully unprepared for the soul.

James Groopman, MD (2004, p. 23)

This quote exemplifies what many students in graduate leadership programs have said to me over the twenty years of experience that I have had teaching at the university level. The students come with questions and unresolved dilemmas about leading, often dismayed or confused by what they have experienced in the field. Leadership training begins, as do other professional degrees such as law or medicine, in the classroom, and then moves on to internships, or residencies. *Graduates are brimming with information, but maybe not with insight.*

Groopman's quote reminds us of the importance of having both insight and information. Insight often occurs with reflective practice; in the case of many graduate programs, the conceptual learning is manifest in the field where the practice occurs. It is the field where practice allows the conceptual or theoretical foundations to flourish. In the same sense, the conceptual learning about mindfulness takes flight by practicing, where the experiential components may become part of one's practice or occupation. It is the awareness or present moment insight that happens with mindfulness practice that allows for a deeper level of effectiveness for a leader.

This is a book written for leaders—the practitioners, people who aspire to or are leading others. It is written to engage reflection and dialogue about leadership, what it means, and how leaders can thrive in their work instead of leaving it prematurely because of chronic and acute stress, often referred to as burnout. It is intended to be an honest and realistic appraisal of what leaders experience and how the practice of mindfulness can help in the personal and professional lives of leaders. It is my belief that we are all leaders, that we lead from wherever we stand, and that our presence, when we are *truly present*, makes a difference.

The book is written to be dynamic, explaining the *how of practice*, along with the *why*, indicating that it is practice that makes a difference in mindful leadership. In this sense, it is designed to answer how to get from point A to point B, by practicing. There are lots of paradoxes in the concept of mindful leadership—emphasizing *being*, over *doing*. But more about these concepts later.

I write with insights from my own past, reflecting on what did or did not work for the fifteen years that I was a school leader, as assistant principal for five years, and principal, for ten years, all at the high school level. In one of those years, I was supervising principal of two high schools, alternating between the schools every other day, with both schools on Wednesday. Now I have a different vantage point, off the dance floor and on the balcony as Heifetz and Linsky (2002) wrote. The view from the balcony affords a fresh view that I did not have when I was involved in the action of daily leadership.

I write from all I have learned from others: my studies of principals and superintendents who are working in schools, advocating for the success of all students amidst new legislation and changing rules; leadership models and mindfulness practice, now integrated into the concept of mindfulness for leaders, a concept that thrives on, and evolves with practice; and for what is possible within the exciting world of mindful leadership.

This book is written with themes, issues, and emotions that make a difference to leaders. Read it by the issues that *pull you in*, as opposed to a chapter-by-chapter read. Each theme relates to a topic that most can relate to as leaders—these are the topics I thought about while leading, they are the ones that aspiring and practicing leaders bring forward in discussions in class, and the ones that gain traction in professional circles.

The style is conversational, one that may lead to practice, and intended for practitioners. Each concept has an explanation, often with metaphors and examples from the personal narratives I have witnessed or heard over the years, and a reference to how mindfulness helps with a response, or how mindfulness practice can engage another way of being.

Although this book is written from the vantage point of educational leadership, the concepts of leading have crosscutting themes that apply to leaders in a variety of situations and contexts. Inasmuch as the business literature informs educational leadership, it is my belief that the themes facing educational leaders are relevant to leaders in other settings. Mindful practice is the glue that can unite the practice of leadership in purposeful and unique ways.

It is my hope that the words in this book raise in you a belief that your practice of mindfulness can make a difference in your leadership practice—*simple but not easy*, as Jon Kabat-Zinn says. We need leaders who are fully present to take up the challenges of leading mindfully. I invite your partnership with the practice, joining countless others who take advantage of mindful moments throughout the day to cultivate a sense of being in the present moment.

There is joy as well as sorrow in the present moment—we acknowledge all for the gifts each brings to us. The learning is everywhere and the learning is profoundly healing; I say that from experience.

Caryn M. Wells

Acknowledgments

This book was a collective passion of energy, one that was fueled by several sources: the students in my graduate courses in Educational Leadership who repeatedly talk about their gratitude for learning mindfulness; the pre-eminent teachers I have had in mindfulness: Jon Kabat-Zinn and Saki Santorelli; Self-compassion: Christopher Germer and Kristin Neff; and the joy I have had to be able to learn, practice, and teach these concepts. I have the deepest gratitude for the professors who read and offered feedback for this book: Christine Abbott, Robert Jarski, and James Quinn; and other esteemed colleagues who did the same: Rachel Guinn and Elliott Wells-Reid. Others on my journey who offered their wisdom and encouragement: Karen Bolak, Barry Boyce, Theodore Creighton, Beverly Irby, Daniel Nerad, Joan Richardson, and Mary Beth Wells. I also share the gratitude for an early teacher of guided imagery, one who delivered a message of hope to many women who were struggling to learn to run again: Gail Elliott Patricolo. My thanks to Carlie Wall, extraordinary editor; and Rowman & Littlefield Vice President, Tom Koerner, for his thoughtful and compassionate suggestions for this book. A special thank you to Professor Rosemary Papa, whom I credit for teaching me to learn how to fly. All of these people added to the mosaic that is portrayed in this book-thank you for the mindful moments along this path of writing.

Introduction

WHERE IS THE HOPE?

This book is written to advance the concepts that began with the work of Jon Kabat-Zinn, a scientist who articulated mindfulness meditation to the medical community when, in 1979, he promoted these concepts to the medical community at the University Massachusetts General Hospital. He has continually shown a way where a way of *being* can replace a way of *doing*, to a world that is on overdrive with commitments, instant communication, and where busyness is a national sport. Kabat-Zinn has shown dramatically that there is hope for people to step off the treadmill of constant chatter, preoccupation, and distraction, and enter a world, even if for the briefest amount of time, that allows them to be fully present.

This book presents a conceptualization of mindfulness for leaders, capitalizing on the fascinating work of several pioneers; the foundation is on mindfulness and its constructs, the so-called soft skills that are so important for leaders, concepts such as emotional and social intelligence, the tenets of resonant leadership, along with information on affective neuroscience, which will be explained in future chapters. The trainings, reading, and research made the task of integrating these concepts one that was natural and organic. I continually witnessed how the works of Jon Kabat-Zinn, Daniel Goleman, Richard Boyatzis, Annie McKee, and Richie Davidson seamlessly complemented each concept they articulated to provide insights of how the practice of leadership could relieve stress and improve practice.

The more I practiced, studied, read, listened to graduate students—the aspiring and practicing leaders in education leadership programs—and continued with training in mindfulness, I noticed the inextricable and overwhelming correlations, connections, and insights that they yielded, and how they led to a familiar home—that of *mindfulness practice*.

It is the attitudinal foundation of mindfulness, outlined by Jon Kabat-Zinn (2009) that include nonjudgment, beginner's mind, acceptance, trust, non-striving, and letting go, that are combined with mindfulness prompts of being in the moment, being aware, and compassionate that provide the conceptual foundation for this book. These are qualities that are aligned with emotional and social intelligence, and they make a difference in leadership.

These constructs include elements of emotional and social intelligence (Goleman, 2000; Goleman & Boyatzis, 2008), concepts such as self-awareness, self-regulation, social awareness and relationship management, empathy, attunement, organizational awareness, influence, with emphases on coaching, inspiring, and developing others. The concepts listed above are integrated with resonant leadership (Boyatzis & McKee, 2005), articulating the challenges facing leaders that can result in sacrifice syndrome that may lead to burnout, along with a view of how leaders can avoid burnout and thrive in the workplace with hope and inspiration.

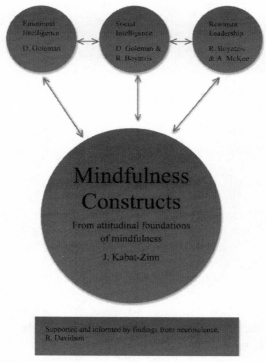

Figure I.1   Mindfulness Constructs

Finally, the works of affective neuroscience show convincing data that demonstrate how people respond to developing mindfulness meditation and provide a path to understanding how the practice can yield positive changes in the brain resulting in stress reduction (Davidson, 2011).

We have a crisis in this country and it is not a crisis of lack of leadership for America's schools; it is a *crisis of not enough leaders who are equipped to deal with the stressors that are an inevitable side of leading*. This book advances the belief that mindfulness practice can yield a powerful outcome for the educational leaders who deal with the perpetual busyness, preoccupation, and distractions that are part of a world that often feels like *"24/7" connectivity*. In this regard, this book provides hope for educational leaders: principals, superintendents, and teacher leaders, along with all of the assistants for these roles.

Why is that? Most leaders have not been prepared for the onslaught of problems they will face in the workplace; consequently they may blame themselves or others for issues that arise instead of looking systemically and internally for means to have a better understanding of and attention to what is happening.

There are concerns for the attrition rate of educational leaders and the unwillingness of many to take up the challenge of leadership. Teachers, the foundation for the usual transformation to the building principalship, are saying in mass numbers that they are not interested in pursuing a job that has burdens and stress that undermines its attractiveness. And many principals, who experience that level of stress, are not eager to trade that level for another by working toward a position as district superintendent.

Then there is the sense of despair that many educational leaders feel as they deal with chronic levels of stress, prompting the concern: *Where is the hope?*

Where is there help for educational leaders who feel they have had enough, that they can no longer provide the direction for their schools and school districts because they have become overwhelmed and exhausted by acute and chronic stress? These leaders have entered a zone of *sacrifice syndrome*, described by Boyatzis and McKee (2005); they described the challenging state of effective leaders who end up feeling exhausted by the unrelenting workload and stress of the job.

What if we were to offer something else for these administrators, other than assistance for finding a new job, or tickets for a weekend away? Just what if we were to offer *hope*? Hope, the word that helps people believe that there is something there for them to *thrive* instead of cope or tolerate, and to stay in the system instead of leaving it? What if we were to say something entirely different to the many leaders who at this moment want to check out of the job where their heart and passion reside?

What if we were to say to them . . .

If you are overwhelmed, you are not alone in these feelings. We have something for you to try; in fact, we have options that can help you and may also help improve your practice as a leader. There are ways to bring relief to how you are feeling in your present situation that may improve your practice as a leader at the same time, and in doing so, give you reasons for staying in the field.

There is hope for leaders to be present with the myriad issues that surround them, viewing problems differently, for the tremendous growth and learning that is possible as one turns into rather than turns away from the problems. By attending to the problems at hand, leaders can view others differently, understanding their perspectives and how they intersect with those of others. When leaders stay with the problems, they learn something about perseverance and resilience, and how to prevail instead of escaping or becoming ill.

Listed in the section on hope in this book are some descriptions of leaders who project hope in their schools and school districts as they work with the mindfulness constructs. Educational leaders who mindfully work to project hope:

- Are fully present for the employees, students, and parents
- Believe in the power of the people in the organization to make all the difference, and consistently communicate that message so all will hear and know
- Encourage others that their work and their lives matter
- Bring others on board by letting them know that they are a team, and that they will respond together to whatever happens

There is help for people who might feel they are at the end of their career, something that can reduce the feelings of isolation and stress while building confidence in effectiveness. And that something is *mindfulness*. Within the practice of mindfulness, leaders can begin to learn another way of *being* that can change their interaction with the problems they are facing, and in so doing, directly impact their schools.

Instead of working harder, or perhaps repeating what they already have done in the past, they can learn a different way, a new way *that is actually a way of being*. Mindfulness affords this different way of responding.

Mindfulness is a practice that can help leaders be fully present in the moment, on purpose, without criticism of self or others. And, by being fully present and developing mindfulness practices, stress can be reduced and leadership effectiveness increased.

The various practices of mindfulness can provide the help and assistance that can reduce physical symptoms while increasing positive health benefits and traits associated with effective leadership—such as being fully present, accepting the reality of what is directly in front of them, and truly listening with patience and nonjudgment to build a stronger network of social and emotional intelligence. *Mindfulness is a vehicle to build human agency in leaders where they are nurtured by practices that can bolster their social and emotional intelligence and increase the qualities that build their sense of effectiveness in areas that matter.*

David Brooks in his book *The Road to Character* reminds us that resume-building skills pale in comparison to the descriptions of what people hope to hear in their eulogies. Although this book cultivates leadership development for readers, it is not about resume building; it is for those qualities that emulate from mindfulness, emotional and social intelligence that most of us would hope to be read and remembered about the legacy of our lives. And for that reason, I declare this passion and dedicate my efforts. If we focus only on skill building without cultivating the *ways of being that cultivate a sense of sangha or community,* we lose the legacy of hope that can fuel leaders in their darkest days.

There is a saying attributed to author Richard Bach (1977) that when paraphrased goes something like this: *In life we teach best what we most need to learn.*

If I am teaching this well, that is the reason.

Part I

THE ART OF MINDFULNESS FOR LEADERS

There is no need for us to speak.
Silence will speak for us.

Ramson Lomatewama, Hopi poet

Chapter 1

Mindfulness for Leaders

THE STATE OF EDUCATIONAL LEADERSHIP

There is an expression in the world of boating that may apply to the situations in which many educational leaders find themselves. The saying goes, "What are the two happiest days in a boat owner's life?" The answer: "The day he gets the boat, and the day he sells it." Leaders may find themselves in a similar position. The happiest day may be in getting that position as a leader, with all the joy and possibility that it may bring. Then the "honeymoon" may be over soon, with resulting frustration, fatigue, and challenge.

What is there to hope or wish for? Maybe the day they walk away from the job—it's a story that is heard countless times in quiet conversations, professional organizations, or stories passed from one leader to another. These are the conversations that go on to report things such as the endless list of *"When I leave this job I'll never miss . . ."* and there is the listing of job duties that are fraught with challenge, stress, and conflict.

Educational leaders are depicted in the media daily, with stories of accountability, the posting of student test scores and achievement levels, budget woes, and issues related to bargaining wages for the employee groups in the district. Legislative mandates also take up considerable time as leaders respond to new initiatives calling for new and different skills and actions. The research concerning school leaders indicates that they have always been involved with stressful work; however, the literature is revealing that the stress levels are increasing for practicing principals (Cooley & Shen, 2003; Grubb & Flessa, 2006; Louis, et al., 2010; Sytsma, 2009).

Boyatzis and McKee (2005) offer insights into the world of organizational leaders that have application for educational leaders. They point to the levels of chronic and acute stress that begin to take their toll on leaders, citing

3

Text Box 1.1

> Many of the students in the graduate educational leadership classes I teach tell me that their first position to leadership was as an interim, when a school leader was out for a health leave. These leaves are a common occurrence as health or physical symptoms manifest during times of intense stress. The leaders who opt out for a while often feel they are buying time to restore and renew, only to reenter the same stress that they left, usually with the same coping skills they had when they left. These coping mechanisms are often woefully inadequate to keep pace with the daily stress. Many leaders describe getting up to one hundred e-mail messages a day, all generally demanding more than a quick reply, one that is written in narrative, not simply a "yes" or "no" answer. Somehow there is a need to push a proverbial pause button while still effectively responding to the problems at hand.

descriptions of effective leaders who give so much of themselves that they begin to burn out emotionally. Effective school leaders are prey to the same type of reaction.

Educational leaders are concerned for the new teacher evaluation standards that rely heavily on student achievement, the shrinking pool of resources—human and financial, the level of constant interruption, and what might feel like endless meetings. They also discuss concerns for their personal lives, knowing that they need time to exercise, be with families, and engage in recreational do activities, but their schedules are so crowded that they are unable to find time to get to activities that can renew and nourish them.

Educational leaders receive text messages from people in their organizations long after the school day is over, asking them to respond to issues that have emerged since they left the building with the expectation that they work into the evening session to resolve issues and settle concerns. The e-mail messages from parents often require some investigation to gain insight into the stated concern, with complete answers to fully update and respond to the issue at hand.

What Is Mindfulness and How Does It Relate to the Stress-Filled World of School Leaders?

This book will articulate what mindfulness is and how it can reduce the stress levels of school leaders, assist in the effectiveness of the leader, help promote a sense of renewal and resilience, and hopefully, give leaders reasons to stay the course and continue to serve as building leaders. Smalley and Winston (2010) reported, "Mindfulness may be thought of as a state of consciousness, one characterized by attention to present experience with a stance of open curiosity. It is a quality of attention that can be brought to any experience" (p. xvi). Hence, people can be mindful during yoga, meditation, walking, or any walk in nature, for example. It simply means an intention to pay attention to the present moment.

Jon Kabat-Zinn (2005) offered, "Mindfulness can be thought of as moment-to-moment nonjudgmental awareness, cultivated by paying attention in a specific way that is, in the present moment, and as non-reactively, as non-judgmentally, and as openheartedly as possible" (p. 108).

So, as we make sense of these definitions, we may relate by distilling the concepts to mean that *mindfulness is when we intend to pay attention to the present moment without judging self or others.* It means that we push past what may be distracting us to pay attention to what is in front of us.

Mindfulness can be experienced by this deliberate, focused attention, which can happen as school leaders either pause to experience and focus on the moment, or in a formal practice of meditation where the leader settles in to focus on the awareness of the breath, or being aware of the thoughts and feelings that are present in the moment.

Mindfulness can be a way of meditating, a way of listening, a way to enter into some quiet observance of the present moment, or a way to eat, walk, or sit. Mindfulness evokes a quality of intention where one is able to slow down to notice, sense, and feel, as opposed to think, evaluate, or classify issues, people, or events. *Mindfulness can be a way of leading, living, reading, and relating.*

Mindfulness practice helps people learn to pay attention, observe, feel, and notice what is occurring. It also helps people to stay with, rather than try to avoid what is occurring. It offers simplicity of the moment without taking in every detail of a crowded, rushed, and overwhelming landscape. It teaches people how to redirect thoughts that invade the mind, thoughts like regrets of the past or concerns for the "to-do" lists. How? When an interrupting thought surfaces during practice, the person becomes aware of it and just redirects the focus to the breath, for example.

Mindfulness is a practice of quiet. Mindfulness practice has many forms—from the focus on the breath, noting thoughts and feelings as they emerge, observation of sounds, or a body scan in which the observer focuses on the parts of the body, again, just being aware. Again, the *practice is done without judgment or criticism of self or others.* The focus is on what is occurring, just being aware and alert to what is present.

Mindful practice can be cultivated in a discipline of entering into stillness or quiet by taking ordinary moments of life and slowing them down to appreciate, observe, and notice what otherwise might be missed, or only partially observed due to the preoccupation or distraction that most people experience.

Text Box 1.2

Sometimes in class we talk about what mindfulness isn't because people identify with the definitions of *mindlessness* as places where we spend most of our time. Mindlessness can be understood by an example of driving on autopilot only to determine that one has bypassed the intended exit. Or an example of eating a carton of ice cream or a bag of potato chips only to discover that the food has been consumed. Or, another example of mindlessness could be talking on the phone, hanging up, and asking what was the essence of that call. We are often ingrained in mindlessness throughout much of our distracted, overwhelmed, and preoccupied world. Mindlessness can be observed in many of the habits we engage in, whether at work or in our personal lives. Mindfulness is the opposite of mindlessness. It is the deliberate, intentional paying attention on purpose.

The opportunity to slow down a daily experience and attend to it with intention is a mindful moment.

Mindful moments include, paying attention on purpose to the small things and ordinary events in life, by observing, watching, and sensing. So, it is possible to have mindful moments throughout the day in which anyone can push the *pause button*, slow down the relentless activity, and just be in stillness; it is possible to do almost any activity with this focus, such as walking down a hall, washing one's hands, or savoring a cup of coffee or tea. Mindful moments include the intentions of mindfulness practice—it is the deliberate act of slowing down and noticing life as it occurs in the moment.

Mindfulness practice is not about clearing the mind of all thoughts—it allows for one to just be aware of the thoughts and feelings that bombard the mind at rapid fire, noting what these thoughts are, be they thoughts of anger, worry, joy, resentment, etc. As thoughts enter and leave the mind, the person just observes and maybe labels them without analysis, such as work, worry, food, etc.

If mindfulness is the practice of focusing on the breath then when the mind wanders to a new thought, all that is needed is for the person to slowly, and without judgment, bring the awareness back to the breath. Likewise, if the mindfulness practice is on sounds, as soon as the mind starts to wander, the person brings the attention back to the sounds in the room, again without criticism or judgment. It is a time to just be aware, with intention to notice, be aware, and pay attention to what is happening.

The mindfulness practice is a time for calming and slowing the pace of the endless list of agenda items, past regrets, or worries about the future, and just settling in on what is available in the present moment.

Mindful leadership engages a sense of caring and attention by being fully present and in the moment along with the qualities that are important to effective leadership, empathy and nonjudging. Mindful leadership can be cultivated by mindfulness practice.

What Is Mindfulness for Educational Leaders?

Mindfulness for leaders integrates concepts from leadership models with mindfulness.

> *Mindfulness for educational leaders serves the leader and the people in the schools through the practice of being fully present, with qualities of emotional and social intelligence such as listening, not judging self or others, while having compassion for self and others in the organization, constructs that are developed in mindfulness practice.*

> Wells (2015, p. 13)

Educational leaders are engaged in mindfulness practice when they are fully present for all that happens, being able to suspend criticism or judgment while listening and observing. Mindful leadership also involves the observation of the political reality of the job, seeking out what is working and not working to be able to be with the reality, not to ignore or deny it. In this way, mindful leaders pause and allow some room to surround the issues that are at hand in each moment, instead of making snap judgments or overreacting to what is occurring.

🍃 Mindful Pause

The only way to know mindfulness is to experience it; much like riding a bike is only realized through the experience of riding, not reading about it. Mindfulness is understood through practice. So throughout this book, I pause along with you to slow the world down, put the cell phone on airport mode, and settle into the here and now. I invite you to experience this pause along with me. . . . I will be doing the same as soon as I complete writing this.

Let's take a moment to notice what is happening in the present moment. Notice where you are sitting while reading. Just observe. Leave your analysis or evaluation at the door and just settle in to what is occurring in the moment. How? Feel the air on your face. Feel and sense your skin, the air that is circulating around your face and your hands. Take in a deep breath and exhale slowly. Do it again. Just be aware of what you are feeling, sensing, observing in the moment.

This is a mindful pause, one that announces to you that you are experiencing the moment, rather than planning, thinking, or worrying. Settling in for a few moments allows you to step out of the race, for a few moments at a time. I chose the color for these pauses of light blue, like the sky, and the symbol is the cloud, one that allows us to notice as thoughts, emotions, or feelings enter and leave the present moment, much like a cloud. So, we are, in essence, watching—the thoughts of our minds, as they enter and leave, just like clouds enter and leave. One fluffy cloud after another. And sometimes there are rainclouds—we watch them all for the lessons they bring.

Mindful leadership can be observed in a principal who stops to listen mindfully to an argument from a parent, student, or teacher, instead of dominating the conversation or interjecting the next point. It can be seen in a superintendent who is providing a vision for leading by showing compassion and emotional intelligence. It can be witnessed in a teacher leader who is patient and fully present in the moment in chairing a meeting, or attending to a student in crisis. And, it is also inherent in a portrait of leaders who practice being still, listening, and observing what is in the present moment. How does that happen?

Through the practice of mindfulness, various attitudinal foundations described by Jon Kabat-Zinn (2009) such as nonjudging, patience, beginner's mind, trust, nonstriving, acceptance, and letting go are cultivated. With practice and entering into stillness, people are able to create a type of spacious

Mindful Leaders

High Empathy /Low Attention   High Empathy/High Attention

	Mindful Leaders
Caring and Preoccupied- Distracted	Engaged and Interested- Mindful Awareness
Disregarding and Disengaged	Observing and Detached

Low Attention /Low Empathy   High Attention/ Low Empathy

↑ Empathy   → Attention

Figure 1.1   Mindful Leaders

awareness into the things that may go by unnoticed or areas that may have otherwise generated an overreaction. The spaciousness is the opposite of the cluttered, over-processed worlds in which many people live. Spaciousness offers *room* to sense, feel, observe, and notice, as opposed to being bombarded by too much stimulation. Simply put, spaciousness offers a sense of calm and "ah" as opposed to the rushed and overcrowded, jammed agendas and mental clutter.

In figure 1.1, it is easy to see how qualities of empathy and attention relate to effective leadership and mindfulness. Leaders who demonstrate high levels of empathy for employees along with full attention are more likely to be engaged, acting *in the moment* for people in the organization. School leaders who demonstrate high levels of attention with low levels of empathy observe but are detached from others.

School leaders who demonstrate high levels of empathy with low levels of attention either are distracted or preoccupied from those who need their attention. Finally, school leaders who demonstrate low levels of empathy and attention appear disengaged with disregard for their employees.

Interestingly, mindful leadership contains elements that are affective and emotional, perhaps not the concepts that are typically taught in administrative preparation, but they are ones that are always observed on the job. Educational leadership preparation programs deal with complex and important issues such as data analysis, instructional leadership, school law, budgets, research, and other topics. The preparation programs probably do not teach about mindfulness constructs, such as being fully present, with nonjudgmental listening, compassion, and emotional intelligence.

Figure 1.3 conceptualizes mindfulness for leaders. The qualities of social and emotional intelligence that Goleman described are equated with leadership; without them, the focus is more on the managerial aspects of the job. It was Warren Bennis who suggested that managers do things right and leaders do the right things. Managers may be efficient and productive, but without

Qualities of Empathy	Qualities of Attention
Caring	Noticing
Concern for	Listening
No judgment	Being with
No criticism	Observing
Acceptance	Mindful awareness

Figure 1.2

Low Mindfulness/High Management   High Mindfulness and Leadership

Isolated practice More focus on managerial aspects with less on connection, interaction Focus on results-orientation with less involvement with people in the organization Emphasis on analysis, judgment	Compassion, listening to hear, being fully present in the moment, letting go of issues that need to be forgotten, responding instead of reacting to issues, creating spaciousness for people to connect, be, and work, cultivating the culture that allows for compassionate human interactions for people to collaborate and work. Influences others through mindful approach
Reaction, judgment, distracted and preoccupied, low level listening, clutter of ideas; judgment of people, concepts and ideas	High in mindfulness qualities that are not applied in the workplace- separation of the tendencies to enact and apply mindfulness qualities at work. Instead, all of the affective qualities that people observe away from the job do not appear at work. Not high in effective management either.

Low Mindfulness and Leadership   High Mindfulness and Low Management

↑   Leadership   →   Mindfulness

Figure 1.3

including affective elements, there is a loss of the qualities that attract followers and cultivate and build capacity for leadership in others.

Mindful leadership includes social and emotional intelligence qualities. There is a deliberate, intentional focus on being fully present for all that happens in the organization, attending to the political context, and connecting with the people in the organization by listening to hear, not judging or criticizing self or others, and *being with* what happens *as it happens.*

With high levels of expectations for the leaders, and the constant level of scrutiny of leaders' actions and comments, it is easy to see how leaders can fall prey to the chronic, or acute levels of pressure. That is where the practice of mindfulness truly matters; mindfulness bolsters responses to issues rather than a reaction to them. Mindfulness reinforces the concepts and messages like *compassion, listening, being with, nonjudgment* as the default mode instead of the reverse, such as withdrawal, anger, blame, projection, judgment, or a focus that is only on results without regard to human consideration.

What about the isolation and despair that many educational leaders feel? These are leaders whose spirits become dampened or crushed, ones who might feel it is time to retire, move on, accept a different position, or otherwise leave

Text Box 1.3

As I taught the graduate leadership courses, conducted studies of the stress levels of school leaders, and listened to the anecdotal reports of the graduate students who were either aspiring or practicing leaders talk of the types of leadership they practiced or witnessed in the schools, themes of stress and dissatisfaction with leadership examples began to dominate. With one particular study, I along with two research colleagues reviewed the results of a statewide study of school leaders, learning of their high levels of personal stress (Wells, Maxfield, & Klocko, 2011). At that point I realized the need to research deeper into the professional lives of these leaders and also to research means of reducing that stress while improving their leadership skills. So, the push for me was a deeper understanding of what was happening to leaders. I had already been practicing meditation and guided imagery for fifteen years. Intuitively, I knew there was more, when I began to read about and practice mindfulness meditation and Hatha yoga. I ordered CDs by Jon Kabat-Zinn and began what is to this day, a daily commitment of mindfulness practice. I went to retreats, two different mindfulness-based stress reduction (MBSR) classes, an eight-week experiential program of mindfulness meditation, stress reduction, professional seven-day training with Jon Kabat-Zinn and Saki Santorelli, and various other conferences and trainings in self-compassion. I applied for and was granted a sabbatical in mindfulness where I read research, conducted studies, wrote papers, and attended trainings on self-compassion and sessions on the mindfulness. It fascinated me to see how the concepts of mindful practice were integrated with leadership principles, yet the literature of mindfulness for school leaders was largely absent in the literature. Meanwhile, the training in my classes that began years ago with verbal aikido, conflict resolution, and peaceful communication had a new companion—*mindfulness practice.* Eventually I integrated mindfulness in all my classes, and trained the doctoral and medical students at the university in introductory sessions.

Text Box 1.4

Graduate students also describe their hopes that elements of social intelligence were part of the fabric in the culture of their schools and demonstrated by their leaders; descriptors such as empathy, sensitivity, caring, developing others, building a shared vision and energy, team building and championing change. I only rarely hear requests that the principal or superintendent had more technical knowledge; instead, hearing regrets that the leader does not have more knowledge about or interest in working with people. *Working with* is synonymous with *being with* in this regard, a type of being fully present and observant, listening to listen, not just to reply.

what has been their calling. These are the people for whom the practice of mindfulness could impact the feelings associated with the stress, all the while bolstering the effectiveness of being the leader. The expectations for leaders are high, as people look for inspiration from them.

When people are asked about a leader who inspired them—the answer is often a reference to a parent, as opposed to a leader in a professional setting. Instead, people often define what is missing in their leaders: empathy, sensitivity, listening, influence, coaching and mentoring, inspiration, teamwork—all concepts included in the definition of social intelligence (Goleman & Boyatzis, 2008). People also describe what qualities they want in their leaders: self-awareness, flexibility, optimism, initiative, and transparency, elements of emotional intelligence (Goleman, Boyatzis, & McKee, 2002).

How Does Mindful Leadership Happen Through Mindfulness Practice?

Mindful leadership is shaped and supported by mindful practice. As leaders push the pause button and settle into stillness with mindfulness practice, they learn to suspend feelings of criticism and judgment. When this occurs, the thoughts and feelings of preoccupation and distraction give way to being in the moment without criticism or judgment, allowing for the growth of acceptance and compassion. There is a sense of being more fully in the moment to appreciate what people are saying with more clarity and curiosity. It is difficult to push the pause button when the pace is frantic and the "to-do" list keeps growing. Mindfulness practice allows for the leader to focus on what is happening in the moment.

Research reports have correlated mindful practice with decreased anxiety, blood pressure, and depression; mindfulness has also been correlated with increased immune support and memory functioning, as well as being able to be more fully present, with caring and nonjudgment. As leaders allow themselves permission to practice mindfulness, even for short periods of time, interesting changes begin to occur with a shift in perspective. Jon Kabat-Zinn (2009) related that in as little as ten minutes a day for eight weeks, changes begin to happen in the brain that can be observed in fMRIs. These changes promote healing in the body and they are a source of renewal.

People practicing mindfulness learn to be able to suspend judgment and criticism—why? The directions in mindfulness practice are to pay attention to the present moment, without judgment or criticism. With time, the judgments and criticism wane as attention to the present moment increases. Kabat-Zinn describes these practices as simple but not easy.

WHY IS MINDFUL LEADERSHIP IMPORTANT?

The personal narratives of school leaders indicate that their world is one that includes both joy and stress. The joy involves the passion of the calling in education and the positive energy of being with students. Stress, however, can drain the energy and life from a principal, leaving the leader with burnout or the feeling that the job is impossible.

The stress can overwhelm the principal whose day begins before dawn and goes well into the night, with all the evening events, meetings, and athletic contests. Weekends are times for additional athletic events, scholastic competitions, concerts, plays, and dances. The *"24/7" connectivity* with long e-mail messages, texts and phone calls, and meetings mean that *evenings are the new workday.*

Superintendents experience a similar, unrelenting pace with calls from constituents in the community, as well as parents, students, and faculty within the district. Additionally, superintendents are responsible for communicating the success of the entire district to the school board and educational community, preparing financial, educational, and other related reports. When does the workday begin and end? The workdays are blurred, without a formal start and ending, with weekend appearances and events part of the expectation for an appearance, participation, or speech.

Teacher leaders provide direction and guidance for their peers, whether by informal or formal roles. They may or may not have classrooms of their own, but they are inextricably tied to student growth and achievement. Teacher leaders encounter stress as they work in environments that are continually changing to prepare a group of learners for a new world of competition and demand, all typically with diminished resources and larger classrooms.

The teachers have classes that are filled with students that represent the issues facing society, including poverty, depression, anxiety, illness within the family, and all of the distractions and preoccupations that occur from social media. These teachers may be completely overwhelmed by the new legislation that ties teacher evaluation to student test scores.

Student referrals to the office keep school leaders busy; the new requirements of continual instructional rounds and teacher evaluations mean that many of the school-day meetings are now pushed until after school. When the school is cleared, many educational leaders begin the process of attending after school meetings, answering phone calls, e-mail messages, and preparing for after-school events.

Concern has been raised for the attrition rates of principals and superintendents, and who will be willing to take their place, given the unrelenting schedules, pressures, and often lack of financial incentives they face (Kelley & Peterson, 2007; Winter, Rinehart, Keely & Bjork, 2007). Mindfulness practice is a direct response to the high levels of stress, and mindful leadership provides a way of being that may increase a sense of hope, rather than despair, along with a variety of tendencies that equate to effectiveness as a leader. The mindfulness practice provides a means to pause and allow stillness in a world that is crowded with agenda items, endless meetings, and interruptions.

As leaders work to stay the course with regard to these stressful and unrelenting schedules, they may experience a cycle of cynicism, feeling of inefficiency, depersonalization, all symptoms of burnout (Maslach & Leiter, 2008). Leaders who experience burnout are in a cycle of what Boyatzis and McKee (2005) referred to as the sacrifice syndrome, characterized, in part, by exhaustion, problems with sleeping, increased caffeine or alcohol use, frustrations, and numerous physical or emotional symptoms.

Mindfulness helps with the high levels of stress that leaders face, providing new options for being with those issues rather than trying to avoid them or inadvertently escalate them as pressures increase and boiling point has reached a limit. Mindfulness practice contributes to stress reduction. As leaders learn to sit and be with problems, the focus is on *awareness* and *acceptance*, as opposed to denial of what is happening in the school environment. This concept may seem counterintuitive because the most likely response might be one of avoidance, such as "*I don't want to experience this problem, that situation, or another issue. I am at my limit.*"

Acceptance of problems may not seem like something most people would choose. However, accepting a situation for *what it is* does not mean passive resignation; it means looking directly into a problem and recognizing it for what it is, without veils or deception. It means choosing to allow what is already there to be seen, or heard, or felt, for what it is, instead of resisting.

❧ Mindful Pause

I am pausing here for another mindful pause—this time to take a few moments to see what is in front of you and accepting it for its reality, as opposed to fighting, denying, or ignoring what is there to be observed, felt, or witnessed. A longer practice is in the Appendix in the area titled *Being in the Moment.* Practice with me as I take this pause . . .

> *Let's take a few moments and just settle in, allowing the gift of time to slow down your world and allow yourself to enter into stillness. Feel what it is like to be totally present for this moment, without judgment or criticism. Just notice what is there to be observed, acknowledging and feeling what is there to be felt. Take notice of your thoughts, feelings, and emotions. Just be aware of them and let them enter and leave your mind like the clouds in the sky, entering for the briefest of moments, and moving on, a continual cycle of feelings and emotions. If you notice that you are developing a storyline*

about these thoughts, just acknowledge that and return without criticism to the present moment.

Allow yourself to sense what you are feeling with acceptance for what is there. This may take a type of intention to be fully present for the reality of one's world, especially when we might be hoping for another reality, or ending. Instead, just allow and notice if you experience a type of peace that is possible without resisting or fighting your thoughts or emotions. Take another deep breath and return to your reading.

When I fight the reality of a situation, it is a lot of work—it is stressful and anxiety provoking. When I surrender to what is there in front of me, I find that I can gain new insights that help me to find a path of resolution. Accepting allows me to have a different kind of strength, one that resisting does not yield.

MINDFUL LEADERSHIP IS:

Instead of	Mindful Leadership Approaches	Instead of acting
Unaware; not seeing the reality of the situation	←Acceptance→	Blaming others
Preoccupied or distracted	←Awareness→	Refusing to accept reality
Regretting the past	←Being Fully Present→	Worrying about tomorrow
Not caring or listening to someone in need	←Compassion→	Judging + criticism
Not caring enough to be interested	←Letting Go→	Holding on
Disregarding	←Listening→	Interrupting or telling your story
Not observing or being aware of a situation not on the 'radar screen'	←Patience→	Lashing out
Denying; avoiding	←Responding→	Angry outburst; reacting
Disbelief; disregard	←Trust→	Duplicity; Not doing what you say

Figure 1.4

Mindful attention means paying attention, on purpose to what is surfacing in the moment, not avoiding or resisting the reality, which could make it worse. By paying attention to the issue or challenge, administrators *sit with* or *face* the issue, paying attention to the political reality at the time. Mindfulness does not make problems disappear; it allows for the learning that each problem brings. Acceptance, when practiced mindfully, allows for a type of release of understanding through the sensing, feeling modes of being.

An expression in mindfulness is about accepting the reality of what is, which is illustrated in a poem by the ancient Sufi poet Rumi who suggested that people welcome all that comes to the door of experience, acknowledging that there are lessons in all that life offers. The challenges may test, throw, irritate, and leave leaders unsure of what to do. Sitting in mindfulness practice helps leaders gain perspective and insights.

Heifetz and Linsky (2002) referred to the dangers of leading and helping leaders learn the basics in "staying alive through the dangers of leading" in a book that includes that phrase as part of its title. They recommended that leaders get some distance in understanding the problem at hand, from a distance that they refer to as *looking from the balcony as opposed to the dance floor*. Being with the problem, instead of rushing in to solve it takes patience. Mindfulness practice reinforces the ability to *be with*, paying attention to the political reality of the moment, without trying to distort or change it. From observing the reality, leaders can make progress in attending to it. The practice of mindfulness helps cultivate the view from the balcony.

How Does Mindfulness Help with Leadership?

It is the deliberate sitting without judgment or criticism that allows for new insights and possibilities to emerge. As leaders practice mindfulness they develop a variety of traits that are conducive to effective leading—affect, attention, a sense of caring, nonjudging, listening, and compassion. It is the practice of mindfulness that slows down the world of the leader, allowing for the development of the tendencies that are admired and appreciated by people in the organization, tendencies that Boyatzis and McKee (2005) referred to as resonant leadership, where leaders inspire others and cultivate hope, compassion, and mindfulness.

Papa, English, Davidson, Culver, and Brown (2013) offered, "Leadership is in the end a human construct" (p. 33). It is the human construct that makes a huge difference to the people in the organization, one that is longed for, respected, and prized. The human constructs are the affective dimensions of leadership.

How Mindfulness Constructs Relate to Leadership Action

Leaders are involved in myriad actions each day, supporting a forward motion to impact change in the organization, hiring and evaluating professional and support staff, creating and sustaining a vision, helping to resolve conflict, and working toward improved outcomes, whether it be for profit or nonprofit. People look to leaders for direction and support and notice how the leader behaves, communicates, and listens; in short, leaders' actions are on constant display for the people in the organization.

The work that leaders complete is like reading a list of verbs—all imply action. Leaders inspire, influence, evaluate, direct, encourage, or initiate in the organization. These actions are a list of what can be referred to as *ways of doing*, as opposed to what is associated with mindfulness, or *ways of being*.

It may seem incongruous at first to see how effective leadership can be associated with a way of being; this is one of the paradoxes of mindful leadership, and it can best be illustrated by reviewing some of the constructs of mindfulness and analyzing how the various elements relate to the actions of leadership.

Mindful leadership constructs such as letting go, patience, trust, acceptance, nonstriving, beginner's mind, and nonjudgment are taken from the attitudinal foundation of mindfulness practice of Kabat-Zinn (2009) and are aligned with emotional intelligence, elements such as self-awareness, self-management, social awareness, and relationship management (Goleman, Boyatzis, & McKee, 2002).

For purposes of this book, the attitudinal foundations are explored separately, as constructs of mindfulness, along with the concepts such as compassion, listening, and being fully present, which are cultivated through mindfulness practice. Mindful leadership also includes elements of social intelligence such as empathy, attunement, organizational awareness, influence, developing others, inspiration, and teamwork (Goleman & Boyatzis, 2008). Elements of resonant leadership such as hope, compassion, and mindfulness (Boyatzis & McKee, 2005) provide essential elements of mindful leadership. *The mindfulness constructs that relate to mindful leadership advanced in this book are acceptance, being fully present/awareness, compassion and self-compassion, letting go, listening, nonjudging, nonreactivity, patience, and trust.*

❧ Mindful Pause

The constructs listed above are included in the Appendix with practices to help cultivate and strengthen them. Let's take a break from the reading while I take a break from the writing to practice some of these concepts. When I felt stressed as a high school principal, I found it challenging to feel the peace of the moment. What I felt in a tense moment ranged from concern, worry, anger, anxiety, sadness—there could be a whole range of feelings. I felt my blood pressure climb, and my voice might have answered with a raised pitch. Other times I was better able to be more detached from the emotion. Sometimes, however, the wave took me out to sea. If you feel that way at times, there are things that you can do to focus on responding, instead of reacting. Let's try a sample that reinforces a different type of feeling. I will practice this to stop from my work of writing; it always brings me to a place of peace in the moment . . .

Let's take a moment to settle into the present. Just take a breath, focusing on the air as it enters and leaves your body. Each breath signals a completely new beginning, and each out-breath signals a complete letting go. Feel the next few breaths as you release the old and allow the new to enter. A new breath is a chance to invite the peace of the moment, and each out-breath is a chance to release any feelings of angst. Breathe in that new beginning and breathe out the old concerns or worries. Let the worries leave without criticism or judgment. Allow the quiet to enter. Relax the facial muscles, the throat muscles, and the shoulders. Let the peace enter. Sit in

Table 1.1   Mindfulness Constructs.

Leadership Actions "The Doing"	Mindfulness Constructs That Support Leadership "The Being"
Creating Vision	Awareness, being fully present, patience, listening, trust, acceptance, letting go, nonstriving, beginner's mind
Building Culture	Listening, nonjudgment, trust, acceptance, awareness
Communicating	Listening, awareness, nonjudgment, patience, acceptance, beginner's mind
Influencing	Awareness, compassion, nonjudgment, acceptance, beginner's mind, nonstriving
Getting buy-in	Patience, awareness, nonjudgment, beginner's mind, listening, trust, acceptance
Modeling the change	Being fully present, listening, awareness, acceptance, letting go
Reculturing the organization	Patience, awareness, being fully present, acceptance, trust, beginner's mind
Building collaboration	Being fully present, nonjudgment, compassion, trust, listening
Building capacity within the organization	Compassion, nonjudgment, listening, being fully present, patience, acceptance
Developing common goals	Patience, awareness, listening, being fully present, letting go, beginner's mind
Resolving problems, conflict	Patience, listening, being fully present, awareness, compassion, nonjudgment, letting go
Evaluating performance	Awareness, patience, trust, listening, compassion, letting go
Encouraging transformation	Patience, listening, trust, compassion, awareness, beginner's mind, acceptance

Source: Wells (2015).

> *the quiet, just allowing the stillness to be in your world. Allow the breath to rock you, gently, without forcing it. Just let the natural breath be there for you. This practice can work for you when the pace gets hectic, if you need to moment to settle into quiet, or the tension gets high.*
>
> Cultivating quiet moments takes some practice. Practice allows you to call on a more relaxed state during a time of tension criticism. Let this practice be your friend.

These mindfulness constructs support effective leadership and are aligned with a variety of leadership activities. Leaders are involved with a number of activities that can change the culture and direction of a school; mindfulness constructs can help with the influence important for these activities. Table 1.1 demonstrates that support and influence.

WHERE MINDFULNESS IS TAUGHT AND PRACTICED

Mindfulness is mainstream in the United States, being offered and practiced in for-profit and nonprofit organizations, with attention in the media on a regular basis. It is the topic of documentaries, headlines, magazine articles, and scientific papers. Mindfulness training is widely practiced in hospitals, by the military, in law and medical schools, by police officers, and in corporate offices (Gable, 2014; Gelles, 2015; Hunter, 2013; Kabat-Zinn, 2005).

Mindfulness is being practiced in corporate worlds such as Target, Google, Aetna, Eileen Fisher, General Mills, Twitter, Ford Motor Company, Facebook, and Green Mountain Coffee Roasters (Gelles, 2015; Hunter, 2013). These corporations have adopted specific, targeted training and support for mindfulness practice. Some of these organizations begin meetings in stillness, allowing people to collect themselves and enter the present moment instead of rushing to the meeting, only to get lost in their own continual thread of e-mail or mental messages. Mindfulness has become part of the corporate culture in these organizations.

Medical schools also provide training in mindfulness for their medical students who experience incredible stress and other deleterious effects such as suicidal ideation, drug or alcohol abuse, anxiety, or depression (Gable, 2014; Rosenzweig, et al., 2003). Krasner et al., (2009) began a program in mindfulness for physicians to work with the high levels or stress and burnout that they encounter, with results that indicated stress results being lowered with greater levels of resilience.

The burnout rate among physicians has alarming numbers; Shanafelt, Sloan, and Habermann (2003) related numerous studies showing that 30–60 percent of practicing physicians reported signs of burnout. The burnout number is not known for educational leaders, although analysts have indicated that it is increasingly difficult to convince teachers to take up the role of school administration (Howley, Andrianaivo, & Perry, 2005).

Schools across the United States are offering mindfulness training to their students, with reports of calmness, kindness, focused attention, self-regulation, prosocial behavior, and reduced stress and burnout for teachers (Flook et al., 2013; Flook et al., 2015). Training teachers in mindfulness practice is available in a variety of programs (Jennings, 2015; Rechtschaffen, 2014). Teachers who teach mindfulness are reporting students with increased attention to learning and kindness toward each other.

Despite these advances in offering mindfulness in business, medicine, law, the military and noncivilian roles, there is little in the literature to describe or advance the changes in preparing educational leaders for the stress they encounter and how mindfulness training may address and bolster the capacity for these leaders to stay in the field and continue to lead.

With the stress levels of school leaders, the loss of educators who are no longer willing to fulfill those roles, and the burgeoning information about the benefits of mindfulness, the time is overdue for the field of educational leadership preparation programs and professional organizations to begin to provide training in mindfulness practice for its aspiring and practicing leaders.

How Does Mindfulness Help with the Current State of Educational Leadership?

The literature is replete with examples of the professional and personal benefits that occur with mindfulness practice. The research also supports the numerous health benefits of meditation (Greeson, 2009). It is the practice that allows for the deepening growth of attributes of being fully present and aware of what happens in the moment, including qualities such as listening, patience, nonjudgment, compassion, self-compassion, and trust, qualities that contribute to effective leadership.

Mindfulness offers an alternative to the frenzy of an overrun schedule. It allows time for a spacious calm with leaders being able to fully invest with what is occurring in the moment instead of thinking of what is ahead of them with the "to-do" list, or living with regrets of yesterday, times where the predicted or hoped-for outcome did not occur. Mindfulness interrupts the endless cycle of doing with a chance to be involved with a sense of *being with, being present*, and *being able* to respond to what is occurring in the moment.

It takes time and practice to develop the space that is needed to just listen and observe, practices that are important for educational leaders—it is not the usual way of rushing, running, or trying to "multitask." Mindfulness offers a vista that is in harmony with people; it is aligned with the features of emotional intelligence, such as self-awareness, self-management, social awareness and relationship management (Goleman, Boyatzis, & McKee, 2002). Sitting in mindful practice, without judgment or criticism also relates to empathy and sensitivity, elements of social intelligence (Goleman & Boyatzis, 2008).

As leaders learn to suspend judgment or criticism they learn to respond with a more deliberate response as opposed to an immediate reaction. They also experience an untangling of the storylines that many people's thoughts tend to engender. Instead of developing a mental storyline of what happened in the past, who is wrong and who is right, or who hurt or offended whom, the emphasis is on sitting, witnessing, and observing, all without judgment of self or others. By observing without judging, there are fewer tendencies for reactivity and escalation of stress.

Boyatzis and McKee (2005) related the problems of leaders who begin with defensive and understandably less-than positive reactions due to the constant state of stress that they face. If the leaders are reactive to the situation, they bring additional stress and angst to the situation; this is the reactive state. Staff members do not view the leaders positively when they are reactive. Mindfulness practice reinforces being able to observe, notice, and be fully present to the situation, allowing some distance between responses.

The emphasis is on being aware of what is happening, without criticism. The practice of observation while suspending judgment brings some breathing room into what otherwise might be a tense situation. The educational leaders are able to respond to the situation as opposed to the immediacy of reacting or overreacting.

KEY CONCEPTS

- Educational leaders face increasingly complex and stressful issues
- Mindfulness, as a means of entering stillness and quiet, can reduce that stress
- Myriad health benefits have been related to the practice of mindfulness
- Mindfulness practice relies on nonjudgment and noncriticism, components that allow people to learn how to observe without blame
- By paying attention, on purpose, to the present moment, leaders develop the ability to observe, sense, and notice, being fully present for the people in the school or school district

- Concerns have been raised for the attrition rates of principals, with special attention related to the "24/7" connectivity that their work demands
- Mindfulness leadership, as conceptualized in this book, includes the constructs of mindfulness such as acceptance, awareness, being fully present, compassion/self-compassion, letting go, listening, nonjudgment, nonreactivity, patience, and trust
- Mindfulness for educational leaders projects a new way of being, one that provides hope and influence for the people in the schools
- Mindfulness programs exist in the corporate world, medical settings, medical schools, military, police, and schools across the United States

Chapter 2

Understanding Educational Leadership

MINDFUL OR MINDLESS LEADING

Mindlessness can best be understood by the autopilot that many of us experience throughout the day. When people go through the motions of autopilot they remain distracted and preoccupied. Considering the daily life of a school leader, it is easy to see how and why the leader can be distracted—there is simply too much happening too fast, at an unrelenting pace. Mindlessness, the opposite of mindfulness, is the unexamined and unconscious actions in which people engage, doing so much on automatic and unquestioning habit (Langer, 1997).

Mindful leaders are fully present, attending and observing what is happening, and responding to the issues at hand. By fully attending, there is a natural tendency to observe what others are doing, what they need, and what they are offering to the organization. By being fully present, the leader is able to be in touch with the workers and the work that takes place, observing and attending in a close and personal way.

Educational leaders have days that flash in front of them, with one activity morphing into the next. Because they are so busy, the leaders often say that their activities and conversations become a blur. It is easy to see how the intense level of activity contributes to the mind being full and preoccupied as opposed to mindful and calm. The mindlessness happens as people are *overexposed* to an unending array of requests, demands, expectations, and conversations. The leaders can feel as if they are often "going through the motions" as they rush from place to place, not intentionally trying to avoid contact, but trying to preserve their own sense of strength, *as they try to anticipate that next activity while immersed in the one in front of them.*

Text Box 2.1

I remember feeling like I was running throughout the day when I was a high school principal, going from hallway, to classroom, to meetings, to lunchroom duty, to the parking lot, more meetings, phone calls, and the list would grow daily until Friday nights, a time of complete exhaustion, usually after a home athletic contest or dance. The mindlessness that I experienced was in the rushing and the automatic responses, as I went from one place to another activity. The sheer volume of expectations meant that, despite trying, I could not carry every detail in my mind, and I did not know how futile that was. My mind was jammed with events, activities, thoughts, worries, and the excitement of the job. I did not know how mindfulness practice could help, and what it would be like to be fully present for what is happening in the moment. Had I known, my life surely would have been different.

How Mindfulness Practice Shows a Way Out of Mindlessness

Mindfulness and mindlessness are opposites. While mindlessness is largely the unconscious act of going through the motions, mindfulness is the deliberate, conscious awareness of what is happening. People relate to a situation of driving in a car, only to suddenly notice missing the familiar exit, thinking, *"How did I suddenly get here?"* This is an example that helps in understanding mindlessness. People go through much of the day on autopilot, without much thought of the present moment. As people pay attention on purpose, they are mindful and aware of what is occurring. Mindfulness practice cultivates the awareness of what is occurring in the present moment.

If the focused attention during a mindfulness practice is on the breath, for example, and the mind starts to wander, entertain a new thought or bodily sensation; when the person practicing becomes aware that the mind has wandered, that person is being mindful and the focus has returned on the present moment.

It takes practice to train the mind to return to the breath. It is a discipline, something that feels awkward and unnatural in the beginning. Many people relate early days of mindfulness practice, thinking that it is impossible to enter into stillness because the mind is too unruly, jumpy, full, like a ping pong ball of constant thoughts, bouncing all over the place.

❤ Mindful Pause

Have you ever noticed how your mind jumps from thought to thought, or emotion to emotion? That's exactly what our minds do. When I notice that my mind is "out on patrol," I practice to bring it back to a place of calm.

Try this along with me; I notice as I write this piece, that my mind wants to take me to a thousand places.

> *Take a moment to settle in to a place of quiet. Watch the thoughts that emerge. Watch the emotions and feelings that emerge. Just observe and label them, such as work, worry, food, etc. Watch the thoughts without developing accompanying stories about them. Let the mind do what it wants, and as it takes on a new thought, just note it and bring it back to your breath. Notice your breath as it enters and leaves the body. When your mind wanders, bring it back to the present, each time without criticism or judgment. Take one deep breath and return to your reading.*

At the conclusion of this practice notice what thoughts and feelings dominated, watching whatever insights seem to occur as a result. I find that this practice is peaceful—it gives me some time to watch the thoughts that my mind is generating. And one benefit besides the feelings of peace, are the insights that emerge.

Text Box 2.2

Mindfulness practice offers something well beyond relaxation meditation or guided imagery where one would visualize a desired state or accomplishment. Relaxation is helpful, to be sure, but it can only do so much as it relates to leadership. With its emphasis on being fully present in the moment and not judging or criticizing, mindfulness is able to help educational leaders begin a path of compassion and self-compassion, with development in emotional and social intelligence. Mindfulness not only helps with stress reduction, its principles align with those of effective leaders, or the *Hard case for soft skills* (Daniel Goleman). I found this to be true for myself. After having a daily practice of guided imagery and mediation that was focused on relaxation, I learned about mindfulness through training. Mindfulness was a catalyst for a changed perspective. That perspective was far beyond relaxation.

With experience of fifteen years as an educational leader, and an earned doctorate in educational administration, it was the mindfulness practice that changed my outlook about leadership. What began to cultivate and matter most to me were the qualities like those that David Brooks described in his book, *The Road to Character*, in which he advocated for more eulogy-type characteristics than the resume-building skills. These are the qualities that mindfulness builds through practice.

The mind seems to have a will of its own, continually taking its owner for a ride. People generally love to think, ponder, and reflect about things. Clearing the mind to just sit in stillness and be aware of the present moment is not something that feels natural to people who are unaccustomed to practicing mindfulness. A source of quiet may prove challenging for some people, especially in the beginning. We live in a noisy world. Once the stillness of the mind is achieved, it can include feelings of deep peace and calm. Other times, however, people can become aware of how much they have missed by not being mindful, experiencing sadness for the many lost moments in life. Mindfulness *allows all emotions to come to the surface* and be acknowledged.

Mindfulness allows people to learn to just *be*, instead of trying to perpetually create or *do*. Jon Kabat-Zinn uses an expression that meditation is *simple but not easy*. It is a simple concept to think of just being present in the present moment without judgment or criticism, a simple practice, one that is challenging to enact. It is challenging because the mind wanders and chatters incessantly, interrupting calm at the most obtrusive moment.

Mindfulness practice helps with an appreciation of the extraordinary that is hidden in the ordinary, often missed, overlooked, or not observed because one is not truly present to be the witness. So the early days of mindfulness practice might reveal joys of learning what it means to be fully present, or anguish to realize what had been missed throughout life. Mindfulness practice teaches people to sit with those feelings as well.

Text Box 2.3

It seems like common sense to say or write that we want leaders who can influence by the way they communicate with people in the schools; leaders who listen, empathize, are fully present, patient, and aware. What might not be immediately evident, however, is how something like a practice of stillness can equate with a radically different way of being, one that *whispers* instead of *shouts*, and models a way that can help others change a culture of an organization. The change can occur as people learn to interact differently with each other—listening, not reacting, showing compassion, and not judging. What also might not be readily apparent is how people can learn how to practice self-care from entering into stillness, and how they might be able to find moments during a workday to pause, stop, and unplug, setting healthier boundaries that can preserve them and help build resilience.

Mindfulness has done much for me, it changed me—I am a different professor as a result. It is easier to listen, to not react, and to see another point of view. It has allowed me to teach the concepts of mindfulness by practicing it along with the graduate students in my classes. And, I get to hear from them on a regular basis, their gratitude for what mindfulness is doing for them. As I write this tonight, I have received several messages from students, alerting me to articles, trainings, and other information about mindfulness. I relate to their gratitude for learning mindfulness—*they are, in fact, telling my story.*

BEING PRESENT IS A PRESENT

Being fully present for what *is,* is a gift or present to oneself and others. People can remember times when they knew that the person with whom they were talking was distracted, not listening, miles away in thought. Distraction during conversation may also be observed when one has to ask, *"What was that last thing you said? I'm not sure I got it."* Mindful leaders are in the present, and that is a gift or *present* of their presence.

If leaders are not present, where are they? Probably doing what most people typically do—*regretting or thinking about what happened a few moments before or worrying or fretting about what will happen next, being anywhere but in the present moment.* It is elusive to think about being in the moment because it is not where most people reside.

Through mindfulness practice people may begin to reflect about the busyness of their life, realizing how "un-present" they actually are. As people realize the pace of their life, it may be clear of what has been missed, not fully observed, or experienced. There may be regret or sadness of not having been present for much of what has been only superficially experienced in the past. A professional life may include the pursuit of advanced degrees, new positions, and moves to new places. With the focus on what it takes to advance in the work arena with deadlines and projects, there can be a loss of the personal connections that can occur from being fully present in the moment.

School leaders race from event to event; often thinking of the next place they need to be. To be present takes practice and discipline, a gentle reminder to stop and ask *"Where am I in this moment?"* throughout the day. It also means taking a moment to stop during a conversation and focus on that particular moment, being there for everything that happens. The shift to being fully present is not automatic. People often have to remind themselves to be fully present as they go throughout the day; the body might be present—the mind is another story.

THE USUAL COMPLAINTS—WHAT PEOPLE SAY ABOUT THEIR LEADERS

Ask people the question about complaints of their leaders and the reports and adjectives flow; asking leaders about their own leadership with regard to complaints most likely results in a different list. *It has been said that people typically judge others by their actions, and themselves by their intent.* Leaders may describe what they intended to do, or meant to happen; the people in the schools will describe leaders by what happened.

Then, there is memory of the leader, which may be fraught with multiple perspectives—from trying to protect the ego, to denying or avoiding what is quite painful to remember. For all people, memory contains biases, insecurities, and areas hoped for yet not achieved. The explanation of something from the past offers new, different, and exciting versions of what might have been.

The ego might be doing its best to protect with soothing explanations such as *"Well, you were hired to create change,"* or, *"You were leading in a difficult situation."* It is so easy to deny, dilute, obscure, barter another possibility, and otherwise protect and defend one's own position, decisions, history, and accomplishments. The challenge is to face, accept, and listen to what is being said or left unsaid. Mindfulness practice helps with all of that.

Accepting the challenge of problems is not for the purpose of criticism or judgment; it is done for the purpose of being aware, accepting, and being with the problems to learn from them. The good news is that with the practice of mindfulness constructs there is the possibility that the lessons learned are ones that can make a difference in leadership.

Text Box 2.4

With twenty years of teaching graduate educational leadership classes, fifteen years of experience as a leader, and the countless professional meetings and water cooler conversations, I have heard virtually every description of leaders. From "We love her," to "We will not be sad if he leaves" and others in-between, I have grouped the complaints according to a few dominant themes; these in no way describe every leadership possibility, but they do stand out among the various descriptions. Rather than develop some of the vignettes from cases I have heard, I chose to list the general complaints and issues according to themes. It's human nature to read about someone else's leadership case study and say, "Well that is a very different organization, situation, or condition." Or, "That was the personal signature of that person, and it does not relate to me." Perhaps reading a list of complaints or concerns appears more generic, more plausible, and not associated with any one particular person. If that is true, then there could be generalizability where someone might ask, *"Could this be me?"* This list generates a healthy and spirited discussion in class.

Text Box 2.5

This is the list of the *Top Ten Complaints of Leaders* that is the anecdotal compilation of concerns I have heard over twenty years of teaching educational leadership graduate courses. Perhaps you recognize hearing or feeling some of them:

Complaint #1—She doesn't listen to us
Complaint #2—He does not have quality relationships with us
Complaint #3—We are not included in any of the important decisions
Complaint #4—She doesn't communicate with us
Complaint #5—We seem to be stagnating, without direction
Complaint #6—He is unaware of how people feel about him
Complaint #7—She isn't effective as a leader
Complaint #8—The morale is really bad here
Complaint #9—We are afraid of retribution, his evaluations, his temper, etc.
Complaint #10—She has forgotten what it is like to be "us"—a worker, or a teacher here

Leaders may recognize some of these statements as ones they have heard; or even see themselves in some of the descriptions. Even leaders who are considered effective, slip into dissonance with people in the organization when they are under chronic stress (Boyatzis & McKee, 2005).

How Mindfulness Can Help with These Complaints

Mindfulness offers a special training into the *world of being*; the reinforcement of listening, acceptance of what is occurring, being fully present, and attending to what is occurring raises a level of awareness and emotional intelligence, all that serve the people in the organization. As leaders sit with mindfulness practice, they continually follow the expectation of nonjudgment, patience, and being fully present. When leaders enact these constructs, they develop trust among the people in their organizations and trust in their own abilities to lead mindfully.

Mindfulness is not about clearing the mind—it is about watching what is happening in the mind. As such, it is not about trying to "find" an idea, a sound, or a sensation; instead, it is watching the sensations and thoughts that are there to be noticed. It is a time of intention. It is the practice of mindfulness that brings stillness and offers insight into their world. It does not happen overnight, and with practice, the repetitive nature of nonjudgment, reinforces the constructs such as compassion, empathy and nonreactivity.

WHEN KNOWLEDGE ABOUT INSTRUCTION ISN'T ENOUGH

Educational leaders are involved with data analysis, instructional improvement, and focus on improved student achievement for every student. Principals, superintendents, and teacher leaders focus on continual improvement,
bringing others on board with the mission for improvement. Educational
change requires incredible wisdom. There is the understanding of the political networks within the school or the school organization, its culture, and the
history of how the professionals work, learn, and interact with each other.

In short, there are complex, living and dynamic interactions of big people
working on behalf of the younger people—its students. When change is man-
dated, there are natural tendencies to question and even push back the efforts.
The response of the leaders is important to resolving the issues of incredible
transformation facing schools. How are leaders prepared for these changes?

It is one thing to know about instruction—*it's another thing to lead it*.
Leaders are expected to be able to do both. *It is not just about knowing what
should happen, it's also about knowing how to make things happen.* In the
past, there has often been a focus on steps or strategies, techniques to lead.
Mindfulness offers a different perspective, and that is the way of being present with the situations that emerge. Take the example of the instructional
issues in a school. Many people recite the common saying that *people will not
care how much you know until they know how much you care.*

With instructional leadership, just knowing the information about instruction is only one part of the work that is to be accomplished. Knowing about
instruction and learning emphasizes *content*; knowing what to do emphasizes
the *process*. It's the subject or verb phenomenon; the subject needs the verb,
and in the case generated by mindfulness, the verb is one of *being*, such as
being aware, patient, compassionate, nonreactive, for example. Process matters a great deal to the culture of a school or school district.

How much one cares can be measured by reviewing concepts of emotional
and social intelligence, factors such as self-awareness, relationship management, social awareness, self-management, empathy, attunement, organizational awareness, influence, developing and inspiring others, inspiration, and
teamwork (Goleman, 1990; Goleman and Boyatzis, 2008). These concepts
translate to a work environment of caring about people, building human
agency, and influencing its culture.

The constructs of mindfulness such as acceptance, awareness, being in
the moment, compassion, letting go, listening, nonjudgment, patience, and
responding instead of reacting, are foundational to the different way of being.
That *way of being* can contribute to an approach that has a different kind of
power, *the power that supports, influences, and builds capacity in others.*
Without building the investment in others, it is likely that the efforts to bring

those people on board with the instructional initiatives will fall short of their intended goal.

Teachers and educational leaders are called on to enact change in their schools; many of these changes are externally driven. As leaders initiate these changes, there can be pushback from those who are expected to change, with comments that may be interpreted as an attack to the school leader who initiated the call for change. If the school leaders feel attacked, there may be defensive posturing in return. It's a challenging cycle that is not productive to the goals for forward movement. Mindfulness can help with that.

How Mindfulness Can Help with Instructional Leadership and Change

Mindfulness can offer alternatives to the cycles of anger and defensiveness that naturally occur in organizations. Conflict is a natural element in human interaction as people have different perspectives and opinions. Change in any organization is part of the world that can be referred to as the long haul—it is something that can change daily, with one interaction moving into another.

In runner's vocabulary *it is the marathon instead of the sprint.* People have the inherent history of their organization in their memories—there is a storyline that accompanies the history. *Someone wasn't chosen for the role of XYZ; the last principal decided that we were all going to ABC; we have been this way since 1985, etc.*

The storylines of people as they think about what happened in any conversation, meeting, or interaction are subject to the vivid mind wanderings that happen automatically without any prodding or encouragement. The human mind gets to work and often tells its own version of what happened, often finding fault and blame.

An example might be a thought that enters the mind after any encounter; the person begins to remember the details of what occurred, who said what to whom, and with any defensive posturing, the person may begin to create a different recollection of the situation, to prove that the person was right and the other person was wrong. People often look for examples that bolster their own point of view, particularly after an emotional event. Mindfulness can alter those reactions.

Mindfulness, with its emphasis on listening, accepting, and not judging, helps leaders to attend to what people in the organization are saying, feeling, and experiencing. It also helps to break down some of the defensive postures because of the full attention that is given with an intention to be fully present for all that emerges. Mindfulness practice brings some space and perspective to a tense situation or memory. With repeated practice, the constructs of patience and listening, for example, are cultivated. These constructs can be

Text Box 2.6

The introduction to mindfulness during educational leadership classes is one that is easy to do. We begin by talking about the state of leading, and what it involves. The building leaders talk about their passion for the work and their dedication to the students; the conversations quickly turn to the pace of the job, the overwhelming nature of all the details of teacher evaluation, student needs, decreased staff and budgets, increased teaching load, the constant interruptions, unending e-mails with requests and complex questions, the list goes on. *I do not have to teach them about stress—they teach me what it is like in the field.* From there I ask who has heard of mindfulness—usually not many, although that understanding is growing over the past two years. There are many questions about what it includes. I show a brief PowerPoint with some of the conceptual elements of mindfulness and then we begin with about a ten-minute practice. Afterward, I ask the students to talk with each other about what they observed from that practice, and the conversations are quite incredible, everything from the predictable "my mind kept wandering" to comments about how relaxed and peaceful they felt. We generally practice every week, for five to ten minutes, and the students talk openly about how the practice helps them in their professional and personal worlds. We practice a variety of mindfulness meditations—mindfulness of the breath, sounds, thoughts, body scan, or acceptance, for example. We study the constructs such as listening, compassion and self-compassion, and the emotional and social intelligence concepts. We relate the tenets of mindful leadership to the leadership in the schools and school district. By the end of the fourteen-week term, we have some quality practice time in experiencing mindfulness and how it applies to the work in the schools. We also study what is happening with mindfulness in the schools as teachers use stillness and calm to help their students with focused attention and kindness. I hear repeatedly from students that they are grateful for learning mindfulness; they often enter class and ask if we can begin class with practice.

practiced in authentic or actual settings, something very important for educational leaders to consider.

The practice of mindfulness practice has simple and repetitive expectations: *Focus on the present moment; be aware of your breath, your thoughts, sounds in the room or whatever might be the focus of the practice; do not judge or criticize yourself, your thoughts, or others, and if you find yourself doing just that, do not judge the judging; when the mind wanders off, just note the wandering and bring it back to the present moment.*

Text Box 2.7

By the end of the fourteen-week term, we have some quality time in practicing mindfulness. The aspiring and practicing leaders want to know why they haven't learned this before and I relate the story I had heard several years ago from Jon Kabat-Zinn when I asked him something similar. I asked him why academia was so far behind the corporate, medical, and rest of the world, including the military in teaching and providing mindfulness. He answered that it was up to people like others and me to tell the story for our colleagues. That, along with the stories from students, my own history of stress as a leader, and the research studies and papers of administrative stress, led me to the passion of writing, studying, and teaching mindfulness in educational leadership classes. All professors want to believe that the information that they share is making a difference, and is meaningful and relevant. Over the years I have heard, on occasions, some feedback about a concept I taught, with an e-mail or greeting that shares a related point of view. It is always gratifying to get such a message. I have never witnessed anything like what I have experienced since teaching mindfulness. I receive, almost weekly, an article, website, example, app, or something related to mindfulness, usually with a rather joyous, "Have you seen this yet?" type of greeting. And, former students I meet tell me about their practice, what is happening in their schools; the teachers share what they are doing to provide mindfulness experiences for their students. I am witnessing the extraordinary growth of mindfulness in the schools and school districts that represent the students attending classes at my university and the related change of sense of growth that happens as a result.

KEY CONCEPTS

- Educational leaders report feeling preoccupied and distracted by constant interruptions and deadlines
- Mindfulness interrupts the "auto-pilot" that most people feel as they routinely experience their day, often without thinking
- Mindfulness practice helps people to discover life in the present moment, with the intention of paying attention to that moment
- Mindfulness helps people to see how "un-present" they typically are in life, often missing out on what happens in the moment because of worries about the future or regrets of the past
- Mindfulness constructs of acceptance, awareness, being in the moment, compassion, letting go, listening, nonjudgment, nonreactivity, and patience are aligned with social and emotional intelligence

Chapter 3

Problems of Leadership

NONJUDGMENT—AREN'T LEADERS TRAINED TO EVALUATE AND JUDGE?

This concept is another one of those paradoxes of mindfulness. The prompt in mindfulness practice is to sit in the present moment, without judgment and criticism. Leaders evaluate performance on the job, give feedback, and are responsible for seeing the things in the organization that need attention. *So what does it mean, in this context, to not judge?* Nonjudgment allows for a type of objectivity to enter into the present moment.

Mindfulness is the intention to be fully present in the moment. Leaders who are called upon to evaluate can be fully present and aware without being critical and judgmental. This is where emotional intelligence truly helps. Empathic leaders who are in touch with their work force and have relational trust are able to deliver feedback that is accurate and timely without a tone of criticism and judgment.

Mindfulness does not wipe out all feelings, observations, or judgments—people judge and thoughts are automatic. However, with mindfulness, it becomes apparent when one is being critical; at that point the person can work on not judging that judgment. With that, the emphasis returns to being fully present and aware of what is happening.

School leaders can cultivate feelings of observation without harsh judgment. As teachers and principals are being evaluated by student achievement results there are concerns for the perceived judgments that are felt; empathic feedback with inspiration for growth from supervisors is possible when feedback is communicated with compassion and concern. *Mindfulness practice helps illuminate the path for this to happen.*

How Mindfulness Helps with Nonjudgment

Goleman (1990) offered descriptions of leaders who have emotional intelligence. These are the people who are in touch with themselves and others, able to offer guidance and support, without alienating and offering harsh judgments. This description is an art form, one that cultivates the strengths of people while empowering them. Most people can relate to performance feedback that is honest and growth producing. Emotionally intelligent leaders bring empathy and understanding to employees. They are not harshly critical and judgmental of themselves and others.

It is incredibly peaceful to be in nonjudgment. Being in nonjudgment allows for a deeper reflection, and a type of listening that is better aimed at hearing what is being said. Being in judgment all day as a leader is like wearing a heavy coat—it is a burden, one that fosters more dependency than interdependence.

So how would a leader give feedback that would be classified as "nonjudgment" and how would that be developed? Let's take an example that might be applicable to a building principal. One example might be seen with a teacher who is not working effectively with students. This is a situation that needs immediate intervention; student learning is paramount. A principal would be aware of the situation and, if practicing mindful leadership, would be compassionate, a good listener, and patient as professional qualities. It is possible to be compassionate and helpful for the teacher, to help improve teaching skills. The nonjudgment might take the form of understanding the human condition of teaching and how difficult that job is, with the assumption or belief that the teacher wants to improve on behalf of the students. In this sense, it is the approach for improvement that takes more of a supportive approach, coaching the teacher, providing resources, and championing growth. This is a growth plan that is realistic, and could be one of nonjudgment while directing growth. The teacher may feel supported and helped, with the bottom line of improvement on behalf of the students. *This is a win-win solution.*

Conflict: How to Be with It Instead of Attempting to Conquer It

> *Without learning from it, it's like drinking the poison and hoping someone else will die.*

The literature is replete with examples of the conflict endemic to leadership. Heifetz and Linsky (2002) described the dangers of leading, with conflict being at the heart of many of the troubles that leaders encounter. Boyatzis and McKee (2005) revealed the upheavals inherent in leading, indicating that most leaders slip into the state of sacrifice syndrome where they experience exhaustion, typically burnout from the stress of leading.

The literature concerning educational leaders describes the stress and conflict in the schools. It is clear that conflict is a serious problem for educational leaders, as it is for leaders elsewhere. Mindfulness practice helps leaders to work with conflict, as well as help to prevent it. With mindfulness, it is not the absence of conflict that is being reinforced; it is the ability to face, listen without criticism or judgment, understand, and learn from others that is the key.

Daniel Goleman (1990) presented a path for understanding how emotional intelligence responds to conflict. He articulated the importance of getting the conflict out in the open with sensitivity by encouraging listening and inviting dialogue to resolve the issue, advocating for solutions that are win-win. He also discussed the importance of observing conflict before or as it emerges, using tact and diplomacy to respond to the situation.

Mindfulness practice involves direct, in-the-moment observation without judgment. These tendencies are aligned with emotional intelligence. When leaders bring their presence to the conflict with an open and curious, nonjudgmental observation, it is likely to be well received and helpful to peacefully resolving the issue at hand. The leaders, who are able to approach a conflict with this spacious awareness, offer an advantage of peaceful resolution.

❧ Mindful Pause

Conflict is something that most people want to avoid. Leaders are cast in situations of conflict on a daily basis, often throughout the day. When I am in a situation that involves conflict, I sit with the feelings that emerge from the conflict and may practice something like this (a longer practice session is included in the Appendix section of this book). This practice is taken directly from the works of Jon Kabat-Zinn known as Lovingkindness (2009). Try repeating the following phrases:

May I be safe and protected, and free from inner and outer harm. May I be happy and contented. May I be healthy and whole, to whatever degree possible. May I experience ease of well-being.

From there you can hold the picture of someone you deeply love or care about, someone neutral to you, and progress to those with whom you may have a problem, changing the phrases to:

May he/she/they be safe and protected. May he/she/they be happy and contented. May he/she/they be healthy and whole, to whatever degree possible. May he/she/they experience ease of well-being.

Ultimately, you can choose the people at your workplace, expanding it to include all people near and far. By repeating these phrases you are inviting depictions of others in a way that fosters understanding and acceptance. It is the constructs of acceptance, patience, compassion, self-compassion, patience, listening, and being fully present that contribute to feelings associated with freedom from conflict. These feelings are cultivated through mindfulness practice, whether it be meditation, mindful living or leading, or mindful awareness of other people.

How Mindfulness Helps with Conflict

Mindfulness practice teaches observation that helps people learn how to be patient and still. Quiet is often a missing element in our fast-paced, noisy world. Mindfulness cultivates stillness and quiet. Some stillness offers distance in a conflict-laden problem rather than the escalation that often erupts when ego and defensiveness interfere. Allowing for space between and within the conflict is a means to really hear what is being said.

It is mindfulness practice that makes a difference in how people can respond to conflict. The tendencies of just *being with*, nonjudgment, compassion, patience, listening, and nonreactivity play an important part in peacefully resolving conflict. People, who spend quiet time in mindfulness practice, observing and listening, receive a gift of space and it is space that can allow emotional intelligence to surface.

These are tendencies that can contribute to a win-win solution to conflict. *While mindfulness is not a guarantee that conflict will be successfully mediated, it assists in the dynamics that are important to its peaceful resolution.* Mindfulness practice helps people to push a pause button in a tense situation and observe the challenges without escalating them.

Educational Leaders Who Mindfully Work with Conflict

- Listen to and accept what people resisting a concept or challenging an idea are saying
- Resist the urge to interrupt or dominate tense conversations
- Respond to challenging conversations with patience
- Build trust by their demeanor

When Things Go Wrong, or *I Didn't See That One Coming*

Name an occupation where things do not go wrong, where people do not make mistakes. Every occupation includes failure—and the leaders' mistakes are played out in a public arena. They are not alone in the headline notice of what did not work well. Professional athletes' stats are the subject of daily media attention. Included on the screen on baseball stadiums are the batting averages of major league baseball players; hockey players end up in the penalty box, and Olympic skaters or skiers who practice and are coached daily for years, fall and crash during television coverage. These people are the best in their respective field, the ones that others pay to see, and everyone knows that mistakes are part of the journey, with the world watching them stumble.

Leaders' worlds are also in the public forum, with actions, words, and communication being judged, evaluated, and criticized by the employees. These actions are being judged in real time, and leaders are responding in the instant that the crisis has emerged, all without the benefit of any privacy for the problem. The practice of mindfulness provides the foundation for building space around what occurred because of the tendency to be willing to just *be* with it, attend to it, and gain insights about what happened.

Learning to *just be with a situation* does not mean that there is no action; it just means that there is time between what is heard and the reply that is given. Even with the best of intentions, leaders may inadvertently escalate problems in the workplace by trying to forcefully control the situations as they present themselves into the situation. *Mindfulness practice reinforces experiential learning.*

Leadership is learned through experience. There are parallels with leadership and mindfulness—both have conceptual and experiential elements. Both need to be experienced to be learned. Just as it is impossible to truly learn mindfulness from reading about it as opposed to experiencing it, leadership is learned in similar ways. *Experience is a great teacher*—the practice makes clear the process, including what does and does not work in the organization.

With leadership and mindfulness, it is the practice that offers the deeper understanding because there is the personal narrative of that experience, one that reinforces the concepts with the experiences, especially when one is willing to sit with what happened and reflect on it without judgment or criticism to gain perspective. The theory informs practice, and practitioners know that the practice informs the theory.

There is a joke about two men in a sinking boat, when one says to the other, "It still works in theory." With mindfulness, it is the experiential practice that allows for the deep insights and growth. Practitioners live their world in experience, informed by theory, and actualized in a living, breathing, and dynamic environment.

The practice of mindfulness can help leaders deal with problems or failure in their schools or school districts. Leaders will experience problems, conflict, betrayal, and challenges. Mindful leadership presents an opportunity to be fully present in what is occurring, and to find a path for understanding, empathy, and problem resolution. Mindful leaders use emotional intelligence to deal with the problems inherent in the organization; these are traits that are aligned with mindfulness practice.

Heifetz and Linsky (2002) reviewed numerous stories of leaders who responded to challenges in work by being in touch with the employees, listening to their concerns, and being able to provide vision based on these accurate perceptions. It is impossible to focus on the present issues by avoiding them, or denying the problems that occur in the organization.

Boyatzis and McKee (2005) suggested an approach for leaders to understand the context for problems in the workplace. They advocated for being fully present for the workers and cultivating mindfulness on the job. They described mindfulness as developing the same qualities of emotional intelligence, such as what they included in *Primal Intelligence* with first author, Daniel Goleman. These authors described the importance of self-reflection, self-management, social intelligence, and relationship management for leaders, all qualities that they relate to mindfulness.

Leaders are busy, often preoccupied, distracted, and overwhelmed. When issues are brought to the leader, they may or may not garner attention, whether full attention, some attention, or any attention. What happens when the whispers are not heard, the repeated requests for attention, until finally there is angry shouting? Just as an unanswered bell, the unanswered voices may lead to frustration and divide.

Once the loud voices penetrate to the leader, the leader may feel angry or betrayed, emotions that Boyatzis and McKee (2005) described as within the *cycle of sacrifice*. They indicated that effective leaders often give so much of themselves that they are left in a state of exhaustion, one that leads to being

Text Box 3.1

The metaphor for this is what happens when there is a gentle knock at the door—someone inside isn't sure what was heard, thinking, "What was that? I didn't hear the doorbell so no one must be here." The knocking is disregarded. *The message never got through.* Then there is another visitor to the house, this time using the doorbell, but there is so much noise on the inside of the house that that isn't heard either, so the doorbell is also disregarded. Another message delivered to the leader without acknowledgment. The system begins to unravel. The leader had denied hearing anything and missed both the knock and the doorbell. Finally, it might be a petulant messenger, one who shouts, knocks, and rings the doorbell incessantly. Now it is impossible to avoid or deny—the message is too loud. But now the message might be one of emergency with all the banging and yelling, and it might signal that it is too late for action—the cries might be to abandon the house. Or, the action will now be criticized for being unheard for too long. The people bringing the message forward might be angry or feel slighted. Leaders often miss the subtle calls, the more emergent ones, and not respond until it is too late. When the message is missed, the messenger feels angry, unheard, or disrespected. The downward spiral begins and a crisis often ensues.

unresponsive to the volume of demands. This is like the unanswered knock on the door. Boyatzis and McKee referred to this as the *missed wake-up calls.*

Ultimately leaders may feel defensive, blaming others for the problems that exist, instead of looking within. Denial only lasts so long and then the loud banging on the door takes over. Leaders need to respond to what is happening within the organization. The leaning in or facing problems is aligned with mindfulness that is fully present, in the moment, listening, and aware.

How Does Mindfulness Help with Seeing Issues as They Emerge?

Mindfulness practice allows for a new perspective, one that is in tune with people in the organization. How? The practice of mindfulness reinforces just *being with* the present moment, not denying or avoiding it. People who practice mindfulness learn how to become observant and nonjudgmental, tendencies that support building capacity within the organization. And, mindfulness helps when things go wrong because of the tendency to be observant to problems as well as triumphs.

Mindfulness does not mean the absence of problems—the opposite is true, despite the many positive things that mindfulness can yield. Mindfulness accepts the reality of what is happening, be it positive or negative. The significance is that attention to the moment helps to be alert to the political situations in the school. Educational leaders want to avoid what Heifetz and Linsky reported are the dangers of leadership: being judged, evaluated, seduced, attacked by others, betrayed, marginalized, or sidelined. These situations are the reality of leadership.

Jerome Murphy (2011) former Dean of the Harvard's Graduate School of Education referred to the inevitable discomfort in leading and the promise of self-care to deal with the things that go wrong. He advocated for mindfulness to allow for all of the benefits of gaining perspective, being in the moment, and becoming resilient, learning to thrive in the face of problems. Barry Boyce (2011) related numerous examples of the mindfulness tendencies that align with leadership qualities, ones that are present in all varieties of occupations from schools, to non-civilian roles of police and firefighters. Boyce indicated how mindfulness might benefit workers as they learn to listen better, experience less burnout, and improve communication.

WHAT ABOUT FAILURE?

No runs, no hits, some errors . . .

Amy Edmondson of the Harvard Business School shared stories and strategies for learning from failure, as did authors Laurence Weinzimmer and Jim

Text Box 3.2

> When I bring up the subject of failure to my graduate students there is often a collective cringe in the room. Aspiring and practicing leaders alike report that they do not like the word, failure, suggesting other, more acceptable and euphemistic words such as *misstep, miscue, mistake, wrong turn, misspeak, errant thinking, faulty logic, missed opportunity, unresolved problem, organizational issue, minor error, or misunderstanding.* All of those words certainly work to convey the problems that leaders face on the job as their actions receive public scrutiny on a daily basis. Failure sounds harsh, final, and incredibly judgmental to students. Yet, these graduate students certainly describe failure in their schools, theirs or others' actions where most would agree that whatever was attempted failed for whatever reason. *When we study self-compassion, a light shines on failures in a more understanding and compassionate way, allowing for forward motion.*

McConoughey (2013), in their book entitled *The Wisdom of Failure*. These authors described what people maybe do not admit when they are harshly criticizing themselves for what did not work flawlessly, or for the failures, which are extremely personal and problematic.

Weinzimmer and McConoughey reported that failure is not always bad or entirely bad, instead, that it is often good, with ultimately good results, and that leaders must be able to look courageously at what occurred to truly learn from it. Mindful awareness without judgment is the message from mindfulness practice and it helps reinforce the learning from failure.

There is another layer to thinking about failure. Heifetz and Linsky (2002) offered a straightforward message about serious problems in an organization, indicating that leaders almost certainly had a part in creating or contributing to the problem at hand, including the reason why it has not been resolved. These authors indicated that the way to work through the problem is to go *through it*, with accepting the loss or problem and modeling the behavior by engaging in the same things that are expected of all people within the organization.

However, without full awareness and honest appraisal, the possibility of tending to the situation with honesty and full engagement is reduced, if not impossible. A denial of a failed experience does not afford the reflections that full attention affords.

How Mindfulness Helps with Failure

Mindfulness practice can help leaders to deal with failure in numerous ways. First, mindfulness helps prepare people to be in the moment and increase awareness, so the chance of realizing the problems that exist before "failure" happens is increased by the fact that the leader is being observant. Mindfulness is also helpful in dealing with the harsh reality of a failure because of its tendency to promote compassion and self-compassion.

Self-compassion is linked with the ability to gain perspective, acceptance, and the resilience to move forward (Neff, 2011). Mindfulness also helps to simply "sit with" and let either positive or negative emotions to come straight to the front door of awareness. "Sitting with" does not mean inaction, it allows for the space that is needed for reflection and perspective, foundations for movement forward.

Mindfulness practice also allows for compassionate understanding of a difficult situation, bringing positive energy and action without criticism and judgment. Judgment and criticism can be in the form of blame, where others are accused for whatever is wrong, thereby losing the advantage of seeing how one may be part of the situation, and its genesis or resolution.

Likewise, without self-compassion, leaders may blame themselves for everything that has gone wrong, staying in that blame without garnering the energy to move forward. As people reflect honestly about what happened with a problem or failure without criticism or judgment, they are free to move forward with resilience, learning from what did not work and creating new approaches for forward motion.

Mindfulness practice can help in leadership training where people can observe what has occurred in the school or school district, with a compassionate understanding of the forces at will. Culture plays a huge role in being aware and understanding what has occurred in an organization. Schools are learning cultures where learning from failure is important to growth and change; blame and fear can alter how failure is viewed in that organization.

Educational Leaders Who Mindfully Work with Failure

- Realize the common humanity of failure—that no one escapes failing
- Sit with the failure for the insights and lessons that may be learned
- Are resilient, knowing that a "failure" can be the path to a successful resolution
- Accept their limitations and honestly project them, with trust in their own ability to respond
- Are patient with the fact that lessons unfold when they aren't resisted
- Practice self-compassion, understanding the enormous burden and responsibility that accompanies leading

Text Box 3.3

We practice how to begin meetings with a few minutes of stillness in my leadership classes, with guided or unguided mindfulness practice. One of the area schools districts I have worked with recently began a meeting with a guided meditation, played on an app on a smartphone. People report that the few minutes of silence helps them to leave issues of angst outside the room and be more fully present for what is in front of them, and the meetings are productive without or with lessened angry feelings in the room.

LEARNING FROM WHAT DIDN'T WORK

Ask people how they learn best and the usual response is "from experience." Sometimes in life the lesson comes first through that experience, in that sense, as we evolve and grow, *we are continually learning on the job.* Learning from mistakes, whether personal, or observed in others is important to a leader. People may not think of a misstep or mistake as something to be embraced; often it is the opposite with people walking away from or denying the problem. A. G. Lafley, former CEO of Proctor & Gamble viewed mistakes and failures differently, related in an interview with Dillon (2011); he related that his failures were a gift because the most valuable lessons are learned in the most difficult loss. Unfortunately, failure is often viewed so negatively that it is not appreciated for its obvious lessons (Edmondson, 2011).

People often relate, *"Well that didn't work well"* maybe as a point of humor or a recognition or admission of some acknowledgement of a problem. Stating that things didn't work well is easier than to admit something like "Well I failed with that initiative, plan, meeting, etc." Because people often use or hear the expression that something didn't work well, it is helpful to see how that expression relates to mindfulness.

Ultimately, learning from what did not work is possible when there is a willingness to reflect on it with *intention and awareness*, both qualities of mindfulness. It is unlikely for leaders to be aware of what happened in an organization when they deny, blame, avoid, or refuse to look at the reality of the situation. This can happen with problems or successes, as many organizations with successful track records either give themselves too much credit for the success, refuse to look at the myriad causes of the success, or become so overconfident that there is a refusal to believe that anything could be changed for the future (Gino & Pisano, 2011). The refusals to look at failure or success are two sides of the same coin that end with a similar result—*not learning.*

The human ego is protective, and high-achieving leaders want to excel, so it can be challenging to *sit with* or just *be with* an example of something that did not work well. But when a layering of compassion and self-compassion is introduced there can be a transformative nature of disclosure and learning. There can be relief and understanding that is possible from being self-compassionate, without blame or judgment, to gain perspective, not enlist a search party for who or what is to blame.

It is essential to be attentive to what is happening, with acceptance of what is occurring. Acceptance does not mean passive resignation; instead, it is being honest and aware of what is occurring in the present moment, mindfulness qualities. When leaders sit with problems, with honesty and acceptance, insights and learning can occur.

Educational Leaders Who Mindfully Respond to Issues That Did Not Work Well

- Commit to patiently reviewing what happened without their own storyline of who did what to whom
- Avoid blame, criticism and judgment
- Listen for other points of view, encouraging multiple perspectives
- Accept what happened for exposing the path to move forward
- Practice compassion with others who might have contributed to the problem, using emotional intelligence to encourage and enlist the help of all workers to respond to the situation
- Discover ways to let stillness enter the picture for the insights that might be evident

"YOU'RE GONNA NEED A BIGGER BOAT"

There's a scene from the iconic movie *Jaws*, in which the sheriff is out in the water trying to hunt down the killer shark, when things keep going wrong. The sheriff takes a good look at the shark and the damage that is being done to the vessel they are in and says to his comrades in the shark killing expedition, "You're gonna need a bigger boat."

And so it often seems when people look into the eyes of whatever they feel is chasing them that they need "something" else to help them—in educational leadership it may be problems with test scores, the budget, people, or any alleged or real opponent. *If only they had a bigger boat, they could solve the problem, make the problem go away, or perhaps defeat the problems by leaving the scene.* The bigger boat syndrome is seductive—why? It makes the situation appear to be quickly "fixable" by attaining something larger, sleeker, or better in some way.

Mindfulness teaches a different way, and that is the way of being with the issue at hand as opposed to resisting or using force against it. This may seem counterintuitive at first. Educational leaders are trained to take action, solve problems quickly, issue immediate statements of next steps, and so forth. Mindfulness slows down a possible knee-jerk action of concluding that we just need a bigger boat to contain or move away from the problem.

EDUCATIONAL LEADERS WHO MINDFULLY RESPOND TO SITUATIONS THAT SEEM TO NEED A BIGGER BOAT

- Review the situation that is the challenge
- Display patience in the review
- Let go of old ideas or "mental clutter" that is getting in the way of a mindful response
- Accept the reality of the situation at hand as opposed to trying to immediately find the "bigger boat"
- Influence others by articulating a vision that builds the capacity in others to solve the situation at hand

KEY CONCEPTS

- Mindfulness practice is the intentional nonjudgment or noncriticism of self or others; this practice helps educational leaders to give feedback that is constructive and growth producing without being critical
- Leaders face stress and conflict in the workplace; even the most effective leaders can slip into dissonance from exhaustion
- Mindfulness helps school leaders distance themselves from the stress by practicing observation instead of reaction
- Leaders' failures, mistakes, and miscommunications are all played out in front of an audience; mindfulness teaches self-compassion and nonjudgment of these errors, allowing for time to gain insight, awareness, and resilience
- It is easy to miss "wake-up calls" instead of facing them for the insights they bring; mindfulness helps to notice these wake-up calls by being fully present and aware of what is happening—good or bad
- School leaders' history will contain failures—they are part of a common humanity—mindfulness helps to accept what has happened without blame, projection, or denial
- Instead of thinking that the leader just "needs a bigger boat," mindfulness helps to accept a situation, sit with it, and gain insights from it; *the answers are within*

Chapter 4

Turning Inward with Stillness

HOPE

A time without hope is a time of darkness, one in which it is difficult to remember anything but the improbability of seeing a way out of the problem. The educational system is not immune to problems that impact other occupations. The rates of anxiety and depression are common in the workplace with stress-related illness as a leading cause of absence from work, physician visits, and work-related short-term or long-term health claims. Educational leaders experience numerous health-related illnesses and problems (Sorenson, 2007). Despite the stress levels, school leaders are looked upon for the hope they can offer.

Hope is the means for expressing optimism and positive thought. Boyatzis and McKee (2005) viewed hope as being able to attract and bring people along with the vision. Unfortunately, the stress that leaders feel may show up with defensive, abrupt, or angry actions, pushing people away rather than building capacity. *Leaders who lead with hope inspire others to act.*

As educational leaders respond to all of the issues that consume headlines in the media, there is considerable urgency to create and sustain schools that foster the highest learning achievement for every student. School leaders who offer optimism and hope as part of the vision for school improvement can foster a belief in the teachers' abilities to make a vital difference, for the students to be successful, and the school district to thrive. A message of hope, as opposed to one of fear or disillusionment, can help build capacity and collaboration among teachers. In a time of focused attention on bottom line results, it is important to remember the affective qualities that make a positive difference; in short, hope matters.

Leadership may not typically be paired with *hope* as a descriptor of what leaders emulate; some definitions would focus on the action of the leader.

Text Box 4.1

Aspiring and practicing leaders in graduate educational leadership classes involved with authentic case studies often relate them to what they see in their buildings. There are discussions about what the leaders say and do to engage others in the schools. When asked about the evidence of hope that they see communicated in the schools or school district, the result is often a confused glance and questions as to what that means. There appears to be little recognition that hope is part of the message or the culture within the many schools or school districts, at least according to the informal observations of the students in my classes. With discussions and examples there is consensus of the power of projecting hope to the people who work in a school district, especially in difficult or challenging times.

Emulating hope is aligned with leadership attributes, and it can be cultivated through mindfulness practice.

Educational Leaders Who Mindfully Work to Project Hope

- Listen to what people are dealing with in the organization
- Practice being fully present for the employees, students, and parents
- Believe in the power of the teachers—to make all the difference, and consistently communicate that so all will know
- Encourage others that their work and their lives matter
- Show compassion for the starts, stops, and backward motion of any change effort
- Pay attention to what is happening in the organization, being attuned to others who might be marginalized, or disconnected
- Show empathy and sensitivity to others
- Encourage others to not worry about the next agenda or regret actions of the past—*the work is in the present tense*
- Remain patient for the things that will take a great deal of time
- Are able to self-monitor and self-regulate their own emotional response to the situation
- Use the quiet and stillness to gain perspective that allows the leader to continue to move forward

EMOTIONAL INTELLIGENCE

Goleman, Boyatzis, and McKee (2002) defined emotional intelligence as having two categories: personal competence that includes self-awareness and self-management, and social competence that includes social awareness and relationship management. These authors indicated that these competencies are ones that are learned and developed as opposed to being innate. They further explained that emotional intelligence accounts for 85–90 percent of the differences that exist in determining outstanding leaders from average ones.

The emotional intelligence competencies align beautifully with mindful leadership. Goleman, Boyatzis, and McKee (2002) maintained that emotionally intelligent leaders are the ones who create resonance in their organizations. They further asserted that none of the leaders they have studied has all of the competencies although they see strength in several of the competencies. The chart below lists the competencies of emotional intelligence that are aligned with qualities of mindfulness.

All of the qualities of mindfulness serve the competencies of emotional intelligence. It is easy to understand how self-awareness is sharpened when one is present in the moment and aware for everything that arrives at the door of the person, being open to look honestly at what is occurring. Likewise, mindful awareness is a foundation for being able to self-manage. Being able to listen and observe without judgment or criticism is important to social awareness and relationship management. Compassion and patience serve all of the competencies of emotional intelligence.

- Self-awareness—aware of emotions and their effect on others; self-confidence
- Self-management—flexibility, emotional self-control, optimism, achievement, initiative, and transparency
- Social awareness—empathy, service, organizational awareness
- Relationship management—inspiring and developing others; resolving disputes, influencing, creating shared vision and energy, team building, and bolstering change

Leaders who practice mindfulness learn to cultivate qualities that are associated with emotional intelligence, issues that are essential for the preparation of educational leaders. Standards that guide leadership preparation programs

Table 4.1 Emotional Intelligence and Mindful Leadership.

Competencies of Emotional Intelligence*	Qualities of Mindfulness That Serve All Competencies of Emotional Intelligence
Self-awareness	Being in present moment for all that arrives at the door
Self-management	Mindful awareness; listening in stillness
Social awareness	Observing and listening
Relationship management	Listening without judgment
	Patience and trust
	Compassion

*Goleman, Boyatzis, and McKee (2002). *Source*: Wells (2015).

speak to the importance of data analysis, instructional leadership, development of vision and culture, budget and finance, and ethical responses in schools, all essential to the growth of the students and the demands of leaders. Qualities of mindfulness are poised to support the work that the Standards require.

Training of emotional intelligence allows for leaders to grow in self-awareness and self-regulation, essential for the work in which leaders engage. Issues related to emotional intelligence, however, are not always included in educational preparation programs despite the fact that school leaders typically derail because of personal characteristics as opposed to technical or managerial problems (Seyfarth, 2005).

Problems that occur in schools or school districts often gain speed like a snowball rolling downhill; issues are brought forward by complaints, and they speak to the complexity of the work of leaders. The frustration levels and stress of leaders are embroiled in not only the overwhelming nature of the work; they are fueled by the inability of the people, including the leaders, to effectively manage them.

The questions become: *What can be done to effectively resolve the issues as they emerge as well as prevent them from occurring? And what can be done to support the leaders as they enter and navigate the white waters of leading?* Mindfulness provides answers to these questions.

Educational Leaders Who Demonstrate Emotional Intelligence

- Are self-aware, monitoring their actions
- Effectively manage their relationships with the people in the school and school district
- Trust their confidence to make a difference in the workplace
- Exercise flexibility in working with others
- Believe in service to others
- Help to resolve disputes that may occur in the school or school district
- Help to build the energy of the groups in the school, sharing the chance for building a vision
- Demonstrate self-control as issues become difficult
- Continually show empathy and compassion for others in the school
- Accept people for the gifts they bring to the classroom and the school
- Listen to students, teachers, and parents for the insights they share and the importance of their feelings

FINDING INSIGHT IN STILLNESS

It might seem difficult to understand how stillness might lead to insight or understanding. After all, leaders are doers—they talk, direct, move, and transform. That type of success is not typically equated with stillness. People often quickly cover any lapse in communication or quiet, with words, talk, or motion. People are surrounded by noise that often begins in the morning and ends late at night. The morning begins with news headlines, from the television to social media. The fast-paced news of the outside world can quickly shift to the leader's personal and professional headlines—often appearing in the form of requests, expectations, and deadlines.

Silence in the day is rare. In fact, conversations are often crowded and interrupted as people explain their point of view, wish, demand, expectation, or mandate. Silence may be interpreted as a lack of communication where the connection is disrupted or stalled. Meetings are expected to start on time and the agenda is quickly and efficiently projected.

Watch the engagement of the people in your next meeting. Are they watching their cell phones, maintaining a constant flow of personal communication with the outside world? Are they doing the same on their laptops? We are becoming a nation of constant connection or what is referred to as *"24/7" connectivity.* Most people do not experience silence in the day. It has become a world of preoccupation and distraction.

People can learn a lot from stillness. The quiet of mindfulness practice allows people to find a sense of calm, or even sit with anguish, if that is what is in the present moment. Mindfulness practice teaches incredible lessons or insights, and a powerful one is to see the gift of stillness.

Mindfulness practice is intentional, deliberate, and focused. It involves attention to the present moment, not what occurred yesterday, last month, or last year. And it is not focused on what is coming in the future, whether in the next ten minutes or ten days. *People learn to see the insights from stillness, and hear the whispers of the quiet.* Mindfulness is not about chasing all thoughts from the mind, but about paying attention to them, noting what is arriving without judgment or criticism.

When people are focused on the loud distractions of the day they do not hear the inner whispers of the mind. Mindfulness practice assists in the cultivation of insight, awareness, and acceptance of what is, instead of resisting, denying, or avoiding what is happening. It may take practice of mindfulness to make peace with quiet; it may not feel natural at first to sit in stillness as the mind jumps from one thought, worry, concern, or judgment to another, but it is with practice that the benefits can occur.

Educational Leaders Who Cultivate Stillness

- Are able to move from the loud distractions of the day to a place of calm reflection
- Practice self-care by giving themselves permission to enter stillness, even if for moments at a time

- Are patient when conversations go quiet—demonstrating patience to listen to what might otherwise be overlooked
- Are attuned with others when they allow stillness in a group meeting to learn how others feel
- Let go of the need to continually be in the midst of noise, cell phones, or computer interruptions
- Hear what is being conveyed, beyond the noise of the speaking
- Build capacity in others because of not having to continually lead conversations, dominate meetings, or have the first or last word

What if I Am a *Natural* at This? Do I Have to Practice?

This is a question that many people ask about practice. There can be a natural tendency to question just what is so essential about mindfulness practice. Some may feel that they are naturally observing and reflective people, for example, ones who would not necessarily need to sit in stillness to reap its benefits.

Consider the default thinking and acting patterns of people, how often people are elsewhere in thought, not with the person who is talking, for example. We are living in a time of preoccupation and distraction, in which we are often reminded by frequent pleas from public service announcements to pay attention while driving. Mindfulness practice helps people to break a cycle of distracted listening, and pause to hear at a deeper level. It also helps people with personal benefits that are aligned with social and emotional intelligence. Likewise, the social and emotional intelligence factors support professional growth in ways that are equated with leadership qualities.

The studies of mindfulness and its benefits answer the question about the need to engage in practice. Mindfulness is correlated with lowered blood pressure, anxiety, and depression. Increases in optimism, cognitive functioning, and stronger immune function are also aligned with mindfulness practice. When people find a place of quiet within, with the focused attention on the present moment, without criticism of self or others, there is a shift in perspective. These perspectives are not the default in an age of perpetual drive, busyness, and stress.

Our distracted, preoccupied lives do not slow down without intention. People who practice mindfulness will indicate that it is a discipline, one that is challenging. Anyone going through training in mindfulness notices that everyone practices—no one is just telling others what to do; everyone enters into practice together. It takes energy and discipline to practice—the world calls for us to do other things, some urgent, and others not.

We hear reports that people are checking their cell phones over 120 times per day. The level of interruptions in which people engage is constant.

Mindfulness changes that. *Thinking is autopilot—mindfulness is not*; it is cultivated by a willingness to sit and slow down the world, taking advantage of being in the moment for all it has to offer.

It takes willingness and resolve for leaders to agree to give themselves permission to practice mindfulness on a regular basis. But, without it, the default thinking continues with thoughts that typically dart to past regrets and future worries, agenda solving, and the storylines that accompany thinking. Entering into mindfulness practice begins to feel more natural with practice, but anyone with a history of practice will indicate that it takes intention to set the stage for the habit of practice to occur. It is not unlike the intention we set to clean our houses, go to work, do the laundry, and anything else that becomes a habit in our personal lives.

KEY CONCEPTS

- Hope is an incredibly powerful influence that educational leaders can offer. It yields the possibility for optimism and positive outcomes. Mindfulness also teaches that all happenings in life offer insights and learning, and that can be a foundation for hope
- Educational leaders project hope in their schools when they believe in the people and convey that message by words and actions
- The emotional intelligence of leaders contributes to their effectiveness in the workplace
- Mindful awareness is a means for a leader to self-regulate
- Mindfulness qualities are aligned with emotional intelligence: self-awareness, self-management, social awareness, and relationship management
- Effectively attending to problems as they emerge helps school leaders to be fully present to people with concerns
- The stillness of mindfulness is a retreat into discovery, allowing for what is to surface without judgment or criticism, and without giving more attention to preoccupation and distraction
- It is the practice of mindfulness that reinforces nonreactivity and nonjudgment, areas that can sustain leaders in time of conflict
- Mindfulness is a gift that educational leaders give themselves when they make time to sit with, observe, notice, sense, and feel; it moves them away from the continual thread of evaluation, diagnosis, and judgment

Part II

PRACTICING MINDFULNESS
FOR LEADERS

Chapter 5

The Challenges of Being Fully Present

WHAT IF I DON'T WANT TO FACE WHAT IS IN FRONT OF ME, OR, *WAITING FOR A DIFFERENT KIND OF RESPONSE . . .*

Leaders may want to avoid what is directly in front of them, and for good reason. The external forces for change they are initiating might not be well received, they might be headed to facilitate a meeting comprised of an angry group of people with opposing views, or they might have to deliver unpleasant news to a student, parent, or staff member. Conflict is endemic in any organization, and schools are not immune to that level of stress.

Wanting to avoid unpleasant encounters, overwhelming, negative, or stressful situations, is understandable. One difficulty with avoidance is that it means *denying or not seeing what is in the present moment.* And it is in the present moment that leaders learn about the culture, the people, and what is truly happening in the organization. So it is crucial to face the present for the many indicators of what is happening, pleasant or unpleasant.

Heifetz and Linsky (2002) made a powerful and compelling argument for leaders to pay attention to what is occurring in the organization in their book entitled, *Leadership on the Line.* They provided numerous examples of leaders who gained insights about people when they were fully present and listened not with what they thought they already knew, but with openness to see the entire range of experience. They repeatedly demonstrated the importance for leaders to fully attend to the political and cultural aspects of an organization.

How Mindfulness Helps to Face What Is in Front of You

Mindfulness practice reinforces what is happening in the present moment. It teaches a powerful form of attention. For example, one form of practice is the body scan in which the person mentally observes the body from the toes to the top of the head, being aware if there is any pain or other sensation. The directions are to just be aware without analyzing what is being observed. It is precisely this type of experience that reinforces the art of witnessing, sensing, and feeling, as opposed to the "work" that most people do as they continually evaluate, think, or judge.

Mindfulness training teaches a concept that helps people to be aware of the situation that is at hand instead of resisting it. Proverbial wisdom about resistance typically indicates that resisting makes things worse. Leaders who resist seeing what is inside the organization do so at their own peril. Sometimes leaders do not clearly see the larger picture. Heifetz and Linsky (2002) warned that many of the leaders they observed never saw the danger coming before it was too late to respond, an important reason for facing or turning in to all that is in front of the leader—good and bad.

Boyatzis and McKee (2005) referred to similar situations when they described the *wake-up calls* that leaders miss, sometimes never seeing them until it is too late. Mindfulness practice teaches the discipline to be able to give witness to what is happening with the intention of awareness.

BEGINNER'S MIND

In mindfulness, the concept of beginner's mind refers to the ability to see things as if for the first time, without preconceived notions of what things should be like, or what people are accustomed to seeing. The beginner's mind allows for fresh perspectives and insights, as opposed to the common categorizing of the experience. People often see things, as they believe them to be, as opposed to looking at them as if for the first time.

It is human nature to label things, occasions, or events many times before they are even experienced. We often project, expect, label, and determine what we *think* will happen and how we will feel about it. We often have feelings of expectation about almost every encounter—food, people, travel, or life, just to name a few. Leaders may have these filters as they walk through the halls of their organizations.

While there are situations where experience matters a great deal, there are also times where the past experience alters the ability to see the present objectively. For example, there may be a group of people who are reflective and cautious about new initiatives that are being proposed in the school. When these same people question the appropriateness of the initiative, they may be labeled as dissenters, cynics, skeptics, resisters, or saboteurs.

Their current questioning may be lumped together with those who in the past stopped the forward motion of a particular innovation in the school or school district. As a result, there could be an inability to view the current questioning as a source of *energy*, one that is pointing out a valuable resource, hesitation, caution, or better idea. It is challenging to not label or assume intentions of others when we have a "past" and "present" with them.

Changes in any organization are typically reviewed with concerns for what is lost when the change takes place; with loss there is grieving. The same is true in education as people review all of the expectations for growth and change. It is very difficult to people to extricate themselves from past feelings and ways of doing business; instead, the default reactions might dominate. The culture of a school is deeply embedded. In an organization, the history people have with others may alter their perception of them. That is why the view with beginner's eye is such a gift for the leader and the organization.

Educational Leaders Who Mindfully Practice Beginner's Eye

- Are willing to suspend memories or beliefs of the way things are supposed to be or *how they used to be*
- Are being fully in the moment as opposed to living in the past or fretting the future
- Allow new perspectives to emerge
- Listen carefully without judgment or criticism, hearing with a fresh approach
- Attune with others in the school or school district, concerned with how they feel
- Engage all people with input, with the focus on what is essential for new insights
- Believe in the relationships that are established for the unique and ever-changing qualities they may bring to the discussion
- Review challenging conversations for the new insights they bring as opposed to the problems they once yielded; seeing new problems without linking to previous ones
- View one's own problems as they exist in the moment, without over relying on past situations or mental storylines that are created to explain what is occurring

PRACTICE—WHO HAS THE TIME?

The issue of practice takes on several meanings with regard to mindfulness; there is the actual practice of mindfulness where the focus is on stillness and what is happening in the moment. Then there is the actual practice of leadership where leaders can create organizations that have high regard for the people who work there creating a culture of hope by their sense of *being*, places where the leader's presence builds the culture, and builds capacity in others.

First, there is company or community with others who are engaged in mindfulness practice. There is also power in speaking or listening to a common language—in this case, the language of mindfulness with the emphasis on the current moment, where people engage in an inclusive environment of compassion and nonjudgment.

Administrative teams can also use the first few minutes of their meetings to sit in stillness, allowing for the leaders to leave behind all the issues of their respective buildings. They can make a decision, for example, to begin their meetings with a time to settle in and experience some quiet. Stillness before a meeting can allow for time to push the pause button instead of racing in, starting an agenda that is over-packed and possibly contentious.

People who have taken a few minutes to settle in before a meeting often find that their meetings are more productive as a result, with less angst and contentious comments. There is much to be said about *what is not said*—that is, *the silence of the moment.* Sitting in silence allows people to find some peace in the moment and be less attached to their own agenda of what they may want to force to happen. The practice with others may also build a sense of community. There could be several ways to allow for some quiet at the start of a meeting; it would be important to get some buy-in from the people attending the meeting before suggesting the practice. In general, people want their time to be respected and valued. People want to begin and end meetings on time. To generate interest in a peaceful pause before a meeting, the leader could ask people for what they feel contributes to a good meeting. From there, it is possible to introduce how many people feel rushed to attend a meeting, how they race from one place to another without time to even catch their breath. The leader could say that she is proposing a few moments of quiet, for people to settle in, leave the rush from the last location, and bring some calm into their busy day. The leader might state, "Let's take a few moments and settle in before we begin our meeting," allowing for about one minute of quiet for the people in the room. Then, a "Thank you" and the meeting can begin. An example for starting a meeting with a mindful pause is included in the Appendix.

School administrators have little time for themselves during the day or evening. They respond to pressing issues from parents, student, teachers, and staff that fill the day. Paperwork, e-mail messages, and phone calls that need to be returned take up the time when the school day is over and the after-school programs begin. Then, the evening expectations begin. Finding time to exercise, relax with time off, or be involved with personal hobbies, all seem elusive to the round-the-clock schedule of a school leader.

There appears to be no time for anything personal; the time is taken up with professional obligations. Principals indicate that they live with constant interruptions, with little or no time for a personal life, regretting that their work-life balance is compromised. How then, would anyone in a school leadership role believe that there is time for mindfulness practice?

This is another paradox of mindfulness. *It is the time that is taken when there appears to be no time available that pays big dividends.* Jon Kabat-Zinn (2009) made it clear that meditating as little as ten minutes a day for eight weeks can cause significant changes in meditators, ones that can be seen in fMRIs in the brain. Ten minutes. *Even school leaders have ten minutes.*

What happens in the ten minutes of mindfulness practice? Ten minutes allows for the person to clear the mental clutter that has crowded, shouted at, begged for, and obscured the view of the moment. By slowing down, the world opens up, all through the vista of the present moment. When the person focuses on the breath, or the thoughts or feelings, the rest *of the crowded, cluttered world erodes into the world of that moment.*

Not that the crowded world doesn't return—it may return in three seconds, but the practice informs the way of bringing back the focus to the present moment, time and time again. And putting on the proverbial airplane oxygen mask first allows for the leader to then be able to attend to others in need.

❧ Mindful Pause

This passage served as a reminder to me to pause as I write. It's difficult to do in the middle of a busy world, and I understand and live with that reality too—ultimately, it's a decision to be made, with intention to pause. I try and interrupt my days when I notice that my mind is racing or the agenda is getting too full. Sounds impossible? It's not. *It is a habit that is reinforced by trying.* The longer I work with busy school leaders, the more I believe that it is the mindful pause throughout the day that will allow them to be renewed with the chance of staying with the job. Let's practice together; as soon as I complete the typing, I will practice as well. I am feeling the need to slow the world down right now . . .

> *Let's take a few moments to settle in, taking some time to slow the world down and be here now. Just take a few breaths, the kind that interrupt the shallow breathing we often experience when we are pushing ourselves. Right now we are pausing, allowing, and being with the moment at hand. When your mind wanders to the busyness of your world, just gently bring your focus back to the present, allowing the gift of the stillness of the moment to be your guide. The quiet of the moment can reinforce how important it is to unplug throughout the day, to settle into the calm, and to let your breath*

> *restore you. Let yourself experience this feeling, and when you are*
> *ready, return to the reading, or the tasks that await you. You will be*
> *ready for them.*
>
> I don't know about you, but I needed that one. I am finding that the
> mindful pauses throughout this book are reminding me to increase my
> mini-practices throughout the day, something that a busy schedule can
> yield when I intend to make the time, instead of looking for something that
> does not exist. There is never enough time—that is why we make the time
> for practice instead of hoping for it.

Mindfulness practice creates time and space to regain composure and find
a more compassionate understanding of what is occurring in someone's life.
During practice, the prompt is always to avoid judgment and criticism of self
and others. *It is very liberating to be free from the judgments*, allowing for a
more peaceful experience and objective view.

The present moment is so elusive, a concept that may be hard to believe.
For many people, it has always been the next goal, the ever-growing to-do
list, and tomorrow's agenda. Many people go to sleep thinking of what will
occur the next day, with the smartphone plugged in on the nightstand. School
leaders are ambitious people—*they have taken on jobs that others would
never consider*. School leaders often describe the sleepless nights or disrupted
sleep as the problems of the day find a way of saying *"notice me"* even in the
middle of the night. What is the approach to bring a state of calm? *Mindfulness practice.*

School leaders may ask how it is possible to *"just sit there"* with closed
eyes and focus on the present moment, watching the breath. It is possible,
although it may not seem so at first. It is precisely the act of practice that
allows for a leader to let all that is happening around him *just be*, and
for all that is **shouting** for attention to be released in the moment. The
world is loud with noise, requests, and chatter. Schools are full of energy
that is constantly pulsating. Even the happy noise of a school can be
overwhelming.

Then there are the conflicts and problems that find their way to the leader's
door. Leaders describe the noise that envelops them, finding it difficult to zero
in on one conversation at a time. *Why?* It's the conversations of yesterday and
tomorrow that crowd in the present moment. Leaders can feel that there are
so many demands at one time that it is like a constant hum of "white noise"
in the distracted background. Mindfulness practice takes care of the *white
noise in the mind*; it allows for hearing what is in the present moment, without
judgment or criticism.

How Does Mindfulness Help with Finding the Time to Practice?

Through the practice of mindfulness there is a reinforcing element to maintain the practice. People begin to feel the calm of experiencing quiet, something that is reinforcing. *But it may be a realization that mindfulness practice improves the quality of life with stress reduction, while encouraging tendencies associated with effective leadership that could encourage and promote mindfulness practice as a daily event.*

Certainly, not everyone who attempts to practice mindfulness finds instant comfort and calmness. First, mindfulness practice is not a magic wand, and it is not a wand of immediacy; leaders seeking immediate relief might be so bundled with energy that it is hard to slow down and just sit in the moment. It takes time to find the peace described above. Many report early days of meditating and being unsure if they are "doing it correctly."

Then there is the human mind. The expression from the Superman days, "faster than a speeding bullet" is one with which most can relate. That's where the discipline of practice makes a difference. The mind can be beyond full many times when people sit down to enter into stillness with intention. Focusing on the present moment might only last a second, and then the mind takes flight to the future or past again. It takes practice to settle in to the moment, and it is not a linear line of progression. One day may feel like a disaster in practice, and the next might feel as comforting as a warm blanket.

With mindfulness, time becomes the resource, not the enemy. Principals and other school leaders are often experiencing a type of survival to get to the next thing on the to-do list. A practice of mindfulness can reinforce a way to sit with the present moment, and not be preoccupied and distracted by everything that is in the landscape of the busyness.

Mindfulness can be practiced in small amounts of time, anything from mindful moments to larger blocks of time. It's not a question of finding time, because most busy people will say there is no time. Instead *it is a matter of making time.* Some people might choose to begin the day with stillness; others may opt for evening practice. Even busy educational leaders can find a few minutes during the school day. A few minutes in the middle of a busy day can be restorative and calming, one that offers perspective to the day, one in which the busyness and entire landscape and agenda of the day becomes reduced to being in, *just this moment.*

How Mindfulness Practice May Contribute to
Improving Leadership

It takes time to cultivate, but the repeated acts of mindfulness practice support the changes in how people listen, communicate, and trust. As people take time to sit in stillness, insights are developed. *Meetings are often places where much is left unsaid and even more, undone.* Instead of generating action, there can be a lack of productivity in meetings and uneasy or disconcerting feelings that are felt during the communication of ideas. Mindfulness practice encourages different kinds of responses.

For example, if during a meeting, one person is dominating with anger or sarcasm, others are hostage, usually until someone breaks the monologue. The typical response might be one that is louder and slower, as if to point out all that is wrong with what the other person said. Instead of this cascade of discussion, consider how the constructs of mindfulness practice might change the course of dialogue.

While one person is engaged with the initial angry or sarcastic message, others in the room are *listening to hear,* not just to *respond.* As such, they drop the comments of judgment or criticism of self or others, and are patient to learn what the other person is trying to communicate. There may be silence in the room, but not the type of silence that waits for the facilitator of the meeting to move onto the next agenda item, but to learn what the other person is trying to say. *Attempts to understand others in a nonjudgmental, nonreactive manner may help to build relationships and trust.*

Mindfulness practice does not make all rough surfaces smooth; it is not an effort at denying or avoiding what might be a seductive choice that people in an emotionally charged room might want to see happen. Mindfulness practice teaches people to be aware and fully present for whatever emerges in the moment, and that includes rough water. Mindfulness provides a dip into the rough waters by intending to be *with,* noticing the responses, and intending to listen and observe, all without judgment. In this way, the mindfulness practice serves to improve the qualities that relate to effective leadership.

Educational Leaders Who Practice Mindfulness

- Have the benefit of a common experience
- Have a support system when things are difficult or challenging
- Can engage in practice as a group to work on improving that group's sense of collaboration and community
- Attune with others as they practice, building relational trust
- Provide a source of *influence that is quiet, deep, and reflective*
- Coach and encourage mindfulness in others
- Practice the art of the present moment, attending to all that arrives at the door of leadership
- Model mindful listening for others
- Give permission during the workday to make room for the importance of finding stillness
- Demonstrate concern for others during the practice

Text Box 5.1

One of my students indicated that he liked to enter into stillness as he was leaving school, just sitting in his car for a few minutes before the drive home. Others arrive early to sit in their office and feel the peace before the beginning of the day; others stay in the office late in the afternoon for some mindful moments before leaving. It is an individual decision, trying to fit in the method and the time that makes it possible to practice mindfulness. School leaders who are stressed and anxious may otherwise never give themselves permission to stop their world and take a deep breath, exhaling the worries, stress, and pressures. The school leaders who have given themselves permission to find moments of the day to practice mindfulness agree that it is a gift, one in which they are *making time* for themselves.

KEY CONCEPTS

- By being fully present in the moment, educational leaders are able to see what is happening in the school or school district
- Mindfulness teaches a way of accepting what is happening, not as passive resignation, but to gain awareness of *what is*
- Resisting anything makes it worse—mindfulness helps with the awareness to gain insight and perspective
- Mindfulness is not the hunt for the positive—it is the recognition of whatever is in the life of the educational leader—be it positive or negative
- It's not about finding time to practice mindfulness—there is no time for a busy leader; it's about *making time* to practice
- Practicing mindfulness for as little as 10 minutes a day for eight weeks can result in significant changes
- Health benefits such as lowered blood pressure, anxiety, and depression, and increases in optimism and calmness are associated with mindfulness practice
- Principals and school leaders may feel that time is the enemy, not the resource; mindfulness flips that—the time spent in mindfulness *practice becomes the resource*
- Even mindful moments such as taking the time to hit the "pause button" in the middle of the day, allows for a sense of calm and stillness to enter the world of a busy school leader

Chapter 6

Mindfulness Constructs

OVERVIEW

The mindfulness constructs are taken from the attitudinal foundations of mindfulness by Jon Kabat-Zinn (2003), and integrated with the concepts that are cultivated with mindfulness practice. The mindfulness concepts directly relate to emotional and social intelligence by Daniel Goleman (2000), Daniel Goleman and Richard Boyatzis (2008), and resonant leadership, Richard Boyatzis and Annie McKee (2005). The constructs of mindfulness for educational leaders are: acceptance, awareness and being fully present, compassion and self-compassion, letting go, listening, nonreactivity, nonjudging, patience, and trust. The constructs can be best understood by thinking of how they impact school leadership.

These qualities are ones that build capacity, offer hope and a sense of belonging for the people in the organization and they are ones that serve the leader at the same time because they are associated with mindfulness. Although following one of these constructs does not guarantee that others will be followed, the qualities support each other. The constructs demonstrate the traits of mindfulness.

The constructs are interrelated; they overlap, and many are interdependent. As leaders listen with compassion, they are likely to be nonreactive and nonjudging. Likewise, as school leaders are patient and nonreactive, they are likely to promote trust. Leaders gain strength in influence as they emulate the qualities referred to as mindfulness constructs.

As you review these constructs you may begin to see how they are like different paths or entrances into the same room, or perhaps the same house. The constructs promote understanding and peace, qualities that are vitally important for leaders who are dealing with split-second decisions in what often feels embroiled in controversy or conflict. School leaders can use their influence to model an inclusive and harmonious work environment for all in the school or school district.

ACCEPTANCE

Acceptance does not mean being passive about everything that happens. Instead it means facing what is in front of the leader, without denying, rejecting, or downplaying it. It also means accepting without judging or criticizing. Acceptance is a great gift to a leader because it is a symbol of the reality that is occurring. Leaders who do not accept reality are in a precarious position as they try and garner support or encourage people to move forward.

From acceptance of what is, is the possibility for growth in the future. Without first accepting what is, there is no way to build forward movement based on truth. Acceptance can be misunderstood to mean passively resigning to whatever exists in the moment, without working for the changes that need to occur. This is erroneous. *Instead, acceptance means to work past the refusal of not wanting to see what is happening, and sitting with what is occurring, just being with those feelings.* From there, one is able to use those insights for forward motion.

When difficulties arise on the job, leaders often shield themselves from what is happening because of defensive mechanisms and chronic stress (Boyatzis & McKee, 2005). These authors described the problems that leaders experience as they deny the truth and perhaps create another storyline or reality to avoid what is occurring in front of them. It can be a challenge to see one's own reality as a leader; it's always easier to see someone else's karma. We may see another's problems or issues with crystal clarity while ours are obscured from view. There can be at least two realities dependent on the eye of the beholder: *the leader and the rest of the people in the organization.*

The leader often feels the need to push forward regardless of what is happening. *Pushing through regardless of what is happening is the opposite of sitting in stillness to witness what is occurring.* Sitting with the situation allows the time or space for reflective action to occur. This is the kind of information that is critical to a leader's success—being in touch with the political reality of the workplace and the people whose opinions matter, whether the information they are sharing is negative or positive. Leaders who learn to listen to concerns or negative feedback instead of vilifying the messengers are building a culture of trust and collaboration (Fullan, 2001).

Mindfulness offers another alternative—it's the possibility of accepting *what is* instead of *what isn't*, all for the possibility of learning, noticing, observing, sensing, feeling, and understanding. This might seem counterintuitive initially.

People might not want to face what is in front of them, be it, a problem with a coworker, talking with a contractor who had left problems with the building of one's house, a painful tooth that may need a root canal, or any other problem that might surface for someone.

One might argue: *Why do I want to accept what I don't want to experience?* Instead, it might seem easier or more pleasant to deny, avoid, or refuse to acknowledge or deal with the problem. Acceptance is probably not the default when someone is faced with something that is not wanted.

Mindfulness practice teaches the *simplicity of acceptance*—it is the beauty of looking at what exists for all that it is, without excessive analysis, contradiction, or denial. Acceptance can be far easier than denial. *It takes a lot of energy to deny and resist*, and resistance usually makes things worse, taking more energy. It just means slowing down with the pause button to observe and allow what is, to be as it is. Liberating.

Educational Leaders Who Demonstrate Mindful Acceptance

- Practice the art of listening carefully with the intention of finding a common ground
- Observe the people in the school and school district to learn the reality of what is happening in the moment
- Are willing to accept what is occurring in the school or school district as opposed to rejecting, denying, blaming, or projecting
- Find points of entry in conversations that are aligned—seeing the Venn diagram of the situation as opposed to the focus on what does not work
- Accept the issues that divide for the purpose of understanding or developing a compassionate view of what is occurring
- Display a desire to focus on relationships for the purposes of building on and accepting *what is* as opposed to *what is not*
- Look honestly at the current situation in the school or school district—being fully present for all that exists, that is, test scores, budget, evaluations, etc.
- Realize that a goal of leadership is to merge various and multiple points of view—accepting them instead of rejecting

AWARENESS—BEING FULLY PRESENT

Consider how difficult it is to be truly aware of anything when distracted, preoccupied, worried, challenged, or otherwise concerned. It is easy to see why and how it is difficult for school leaders to be fully aware of what is happening in the present. And with this, is the obvious "fall from the cliff" if one cannot fully attend to what is directly in front or off to the side of the leader.

Text Box 6.1

Graduate students in my education leadership classes—the "full-time everything" people, full-time students, workers, parents, and significant others describe frantic missions to accomplish, finish, and go on to the next thing in the "to-do" list. There are times when students come into my class after working in the school all day and say comments like, *"I feel that I cannot catch my breath."* They want to slow down their world but it isn't always obvious what to do. In general, I have learned that people do not know what it means to take care of themselves. The reality that is understood is *busyness.* Our language is often consumed with what seems to be a badge of honor of how busy we are. We often give reports of how busy we are, followed by someone else who can top that level of busyness. Most of us know at a very deep level of understanding that our busyness is not healthy. Jon Kabat-Zinn tells a powerful story that includes a metaphor of people who are so busy climbing each rung of the proverbial ladder of success only to get to the top and realize that they had it against the wrong wall.

Mindfulness helps to focus attention on the present moment, and importantly, to be fully present for it.

School leaders are charged to foster changes within the school and school district. Some of the change efforts are created with their own initiatives and others are fostered by local, state, or national legislation. Then there is the reality of the day-to-day business within the school and school district. Leaders are working for continuous improvement of faculty and students. It is impossible to move forward without a realistic appraisal of what is happening in the present moment. To deny reality is to avoid the gift of truth that is happening in the moment.

To be aware of what is happening in any organization means to be fully present, observing and listening to what others have to say, or *sensing what they are hesitant to say.* School leaders can intuit what is happening in a crowd of people when they are fully present and observing the dynamics of the group. If distracted or pushing for a particular agenda, it is far too easy to miss the pulse of what is occurring. The busyness of school leaders, work against the opportunity to be fully present and fully aware.

Educational Leaders Who Practice Being Aware and Fully Present

- Develop their skills of observing, listening, sensing, and noticing
- Set the intention to *pay attention*
- Want to know what others think, believe, and feel—it matters to them

- Model for others what it means to be there for the good and tough times with their presence
- Are able to set the pause button and focus the attention on what is occurring

COMPASSION AND SELF-COMPASSION

Compassion has been referred to as the action form of empathy, taking it to a higher level. Gilbert (2009) described compassion by a number of attributes that include empathy and nonjudgment, which are qualities of mindfulness. Self-compassion refers to developing the attributes of caring, nonjudgment, and concern for oneself.

Compassion is like fuel to a leader's engine—it *empowers, lifts, and sustains in time of crisis.* Educational leaders probably do not think of compassion as primary in a crisis; they may be solution minded, thinking of what needs to be done to address the problem. Additionally, some leaders may feel that the display of compassion may make one appear weak or uncertain. Compassion probably does not come to mind when one is thinking about leadership, yet it is something that makes a tremendous difference in solving a problem, building capacity, or offering hope to others in the school or school district.

People often find that they are not generally very good at being self-compassionate with the things that didn't go well on the job. Instead of self-compassion, there is self-criticism that may play like a recording without end. People are not often very kind to themselves, blaming or regretting with a harsh voice, repeating over and over again, what could have been different. Many high-achieving people have almost perfectionistic standards and expectations for flawless performance.

We know that schools have strong histories and cultures and the educational leaders are expected to help with transformational change. Leaders are in the public forum, providing the incentives, reason, and vision for change,

Text Box 6.2

One suggestion for people who are being self-critical is to consider answering a simple question: *"How would you talk to a friend or colleague who had a similar story?"* The answer is always the same. *"Well, that would be different. I would understand and would even try to make them feel better about the situation." "Well, how about you?"* And once again, *"That would be different. I should have known better. I should have known what to do."* Self-compassion teaches people to talk to themselves as they would talk to a friend, offering compassionate understanding.

which makes them the recipient of anger and frustration that might accompany the change.

The levels of change that are occurring in schools result in many challenges for the principals and superintendents who are leading them. The challenges often result in stress and problems. Compassion provides an alternative way of looking at the problems. For example, if a school district is undergoing a redistricting due to loss of students, students may be sent to new schools and schools, closed with personnel shifted from one school to another. When the complexities of the situation are addressed, it is clear that many teachers will feel displaced and uncertain of the new school and its culture.

If the teachers were angry or openly sharing their feelings about the closing of one school for another, the leader could frame the situation compassionately. A compassionate view would be one where the views of teachers were taken into consideration, and teachers would be listened to for the suggestions they would bring to the way in which the implementation would take place. A compassionate response would include active listening, responding, communicating, and understanding the unsettling nature of change and how it can manifest in anyone.

Leaders who display compassionate understanding in tense or difficult situations convey a sense of caring and strong leadership. Boyatzis and McKee (2005) linked compassion with hope, important attributes for leaders to attract people during tough times. Hope offers a view of a better outcome, a renewed view that things can be improved.

Self-compassion allows people to move past negative events in life, with recognition for one's part in the difficulty with lenses that understand instead of blame (Germer, 2009). In this manner, self-compassion does not repress or deny what has happened and how we may be part of the problem, but it reduces the tendency for leaders to over-identify with and self-blame for what went wrong (Neff, 2003).

Self-compassion is linked with a view that life conditions are part of an extended human experience, allowing for people to view their problems within the context of a larger community (Birnie, Speca, & Carlson, 2010). Self-compassion contains the elements of being kind instead of harsh with the self in the face of failure or a painful encounter, of seeing the common experience of problems that happens with all humans, and being able to keep perspective without over-identifying with the problem (Neff, 2003).

How could school leaders develop self-compassion, and offer hope in times of conflict? Mindfulness helps with the development of self-compassion. Self-compassion has a number of benefits that apply to qualities of leadership such as patience, acceptance, trust, listening, self-regulation, and empathy.

Educational Leaders Who Practice Mindful Self-Compassion

- Accept that all leadership roles have conflict and problems, and are willing to "*give themselves a break*" with regard to the myth of leading with perfection
- Know that problems or mistakes that are made by leaders are part of the fabric of a common humanity, that all people make mistakes
- Talk to themselves with kindness instead of a harshly critical voice
- Take some time to sit with the natural feelings of disappointment for the insights that they may yield
- Realize that self-compassion is a foundation for resilience
- Develop trust in one's own abilities as leader
- Accept natural limitations of self—not expecting to work without problems
- Are willing to engage in stillness to develop practice in self-compassion
- Show empathy for others who have problems with leadership

Compassion is a gift for others who are recipients and, it turns out that it is also one for the person expressing compassion. Self-compassion is a gift of renewal, and it can be a source of understanding that can help one stay "in the game" of leading and serving. People understand the despair of feeling negatively about oneself; self-compassion changes that.

Text Box 6.3

In class we practice with an activity called "Just like me" where we list some of the characteristics of difficult people or problems in the organization. After we list those problems, we reframe them to seek an alternate understanding of what is going on behind the curtain of what we see expressed in front of us. Hence, someone who is continually arguing in faculty meetings may be understood to perhaps need to be validated. Perhaps the actions of the person may be attributed to their own sense of wanting to belong or be heard. Once the behaviors are reframed, the expression is "*Just like me*" which takes away some of the blame, anger, or resentment that may be held for the person displaying some of the problems we want to eradicate. The graduate students in education leadership courses who begin to practice this often report how they view people differently as a result, and how this view often does something to change what they perceive to be happening. There is a collective wisdom in the room that there is a reciprocal communication among people when tensions and conflicts emerge, and that compassion goes a long way with the peaceful resolution of the same.

LETTING GO

What do leaders hang on to? There may be "old" messages in the e-mail inbox, a repository of the cascading e-mail threads from communications that are no longer needed. Or, there might be, for example, a pile of really interesting books yet to be read. We often hold on to things in an unconscious state. Why is that? Most leaders will say that there is no time to keep the pile of paperwork, electronic messages, and reports to be filed, in check.

Then there are memories and thoughts that fill and inhabit the mind, causing a type of preoccupation or distraction that can interrupt sleep, the focus on meetings or conversations, and otherwise intrude when they are not welcome. The thoughts and feelings can replay on a channel that is on at the most unwelcome times—like the middle of the night, or intruding on an otherwise happy event. Letting go? Yes, but that is often an elusive term.

Invariably as there is talk about the issue of letting go, there may be a reference to holding on, or even hoarding; that descriptor is probably very accurate in terms of what we store in our memories and offices. *We are drowning in data, messages, paper, and general clutter.* Some people panic when they do not have their calendars, cell phones, and computer tablets with them. There was a recent question that was asked on the news as to whether or not someone would leave a plane they had boarded if they had left a smartphone in their car en route on a business trip. This question garnered a lot of discussion about how people feel without the ever-present smartphone and other computer equipment.

How do leaders let go? This is a concept that is foreign to most people— what if we need something in the future and then it is gone, erased, deleted, or trashed? This can cause a feeling of near panic with just the thought of it. Then there are the thoughts that probably no longer serve us, ones that go round and round in the mind, played out in the middle of the night, but we keep putting on like an old, familiar coat. That is until we have a different insight, *"This old coat? It doesn't fit me anymore."* Letting go can be like losing the last ten pounds in a weight loss endeavor—maybe not easy to do, but a result is often, *"Why didn't I do this before?"*

The professional training in mindfulness with Jon Kabat-Zinn and Saki Santorelli asks the participants to join in 36 hours of silence. This length of silence offers an amazing experience of letting go of many of the things we unnecessarily carry around with us. There is something quite remarkable about silence that offers insights that are typically never realized. It may not be easy to allow stillness—it is not our way in the world. However, through the stillness, it becomes easier to let go. And, the good news—it doesn't take a period of 36 hours of silence to experience a shift in perspective about releasing old habits or thoughts. It can begin with dialing down the temperature on the thoughts that are most repetitive, the ones that cause inner turbulence.

As these thoughts bombard the mind, it is an opportunity to note the disturbance and bring the attention back to the present moment. The memory might intrude again in two seconds, with a *"Hey, I was talking to you"* attitude. Just note the thought or feeling and return to the present moment. Over and over again—repetition works.

It is also worth asking what we do to allow the invasive entry into our world. *Can we let go of our smartphones or e-mails for one evening? If not, how about two hours?* People report that their constant connectivity to social media is exhausting, yet many are unable to even think of reducing their time with it, let alone, let go of it for specified times throughout the day or night. It seems that letting go is one of those "simple, but not easy" answers as Jon Kabat-Zinn referred to when he spoke of mindfulness practice. It seems that the answer is embedded in mindfulness.

Letting go involves the release of ideas or things that are often in the past, yet once the person allows the mind wandering to bring them forward, the problems are once again in front and center. It takes patience and discipline to

Text Box 6.4

"What do you have trouble letting go of?" is a question I ask the graduate students in my classes. As we generate a list of so many things, it seems to point to the universal condition of the human experience. We tend to hang on to, instead of letting go of old baggage from the past, or worries that may happen again in the future. People feel some catharsis in first listing what they hang on to, perhaps as motivation to finally let go of it. We ask the question, "What should leaders let go of?" when we talk in class. The students have interesting ideas, based on their own lives and the view that they have of the leaders in their schools. In general there is agreement that we are all in need to letting go of old memories that bind us to a dark past of regrets or problems. Letting go, however, is elusive. First there is confusion in knowing what it means to let go, particularly if we may not have experienced it, or noticed it in others. One means of letting go is to sit in silence, calling into awareness something that no longer fits for someone, watching it come into awareness as a thought or feeling, and watching it leave, much like a cloud that comes into and leaves the awareness. From there, the practice includes observing the issue leaving and, watching if the thought or feeling returns. It takes discipline to consciously let the issue go, something that may take several attempts to practice before it is successful.

finally let go of these troubling memories; they surface at the most inopportune times. Mindfulness allows for leaders to enter into a world of spacious stillness, where there is room and quiet, even in the middle of a busy, loud world. It is a way to learn how to quiet intrusive thoughts.

Educational Leaders Who Mindfully Let Go

* Give themselves permission to not hold on to everything; old feelings, mental clutter, and thoughts that no longer serve them
* Accept what is in the present moment with the purpose of allowing and not rejecting the reality of the situation, regardless of the emotion
* Compassionately view others in the school and school district, without assumptions from the past or worries of the future
* Practice self-compassion to assist in letting go of challenging or hurtful memories
* Agree to give permission to rid the self of what no longer works, or is weighing that person down to be able to respond and move forward
* Trust in one's abilities to lead, despite the past
* Use patience to let go of the issues from the past that interfere with the present moment
* Let go of the issues from the past that might interfere with forming new and more collaborative work environment
* Do not allow the distractions and preoccupations of the past to interfere with the letting go in the present

LISTENING

Practicing mindfulness results in benefits for communication. It isn't automatic but at some point it is possible to stop thinking about the reply in a conversation and focus on what is being heard. How many times do people, perhaps in the spirit of reaching out with understanding during a conversation, quickly remark how they had experienced the same thing, something similar, or knew of someone else who had experienced something similar? The conversation then shifts to another party, with the emphasis off of the person who initiated the conversation. The conversation has shifted and the listening has ended for the person who began the dialogue.

The more people practice mindfulness, the more the focus is on listening, a different experience than what one is accustomed. Now, there is a focused attention *to be with* the person who is talking, instead of the response. People typically listen to respond, thinking less about listening or really attending to what is being conveyed with the message. This happens when people give up the instant replies, or interruptions to be content to sit with, be with, and just observe. And when this happens without judging or criticizing, it is easier to just listen with compassion. Compassionate listening allows for spaciousness or S-P-A-C-E. We learn there is space after listening, like the quiet between the words.

We discover that there is no need to try and tie together the comments with a "bow" or "make everything right." These are liberating concepts. We discover that there is joy in ordinary conversations, as opposed to thinking, *"Hurry up and finish, I've got to go . . ."* or being so distracted that the real message is never heard. As people learn to listen mindfully, there may be remorse for what has been lost over the years when they learn how perpetual busyness or distraction interfered with hearing the content or message, and reflecting on another's story.

People who are fully present and attending are able to hear and understand the context with deeper meaning. Attention can fuel a sense of caring, which may also result in caring in return. The reciprocal nature of these traits is a benefit of mindful leadership. It is a distinct privilege to be able to hear what people are saying, as opposed to missing half of the dialogue and perhaps *the real message.* In one sense, it is almost like awakening to deeper perspectives and first time visual and auditory experiences.

Mindfulness practice reinforces quiet, spacious listening. Spacious listening surrounds the communication with room: room to truly hear what is being said, and room to absorb the message. It is listening to hear as opposed to respond. People often relate to the opposite in which conversations in meetings might simulate "attack and defend" posturing where people dominate meetings with the defense of their own ideas, while others in the room are hostage to the pontificating, or maybe even angry, sarcastic, or hostile comments and arguments. Other times people may persistently hold on to an idea or philosophy without argument or relenting. It can be a war of words,

Text Box 6.5

For the ten years that I was principal, I did my best to listen to every concern and issue, but the overwhelming nature of the job and its frantic pace left me feeling so distracted and preoccupied that I could only half-listen at times, instead of hearing the full context of what was being said. I would listen to one concern with what I termed a "split screen" of attention, listening while thinking of what else occupied my thoughts—usually the unanswered e-mails, people waiting for a return call, a visitor in the office, a letter of recommendation or evaluation that had to be written. It was an endless stream of needs—needing to be in several places at once. I could not keep up with the listening—there was just too much to be heard.

Text Box 6.6

> In class we learn about mindfulness and how the practice reinforces hearing, listening to our own thoughts, and of course, the sounds that are always present, ones that we do not have to strive for, only be aware of and observe without judgment. We practice listening to another person's story without interruption as one example of what it means to truly listen. *We listen, nothing more.* We do not offer statements such as, "Oh, that happened to me, my neighbor, or my in-laws." The directive is to sit and listen, offering the gift of presence or silence. We learn that this type of listening is a unique experience for people, one that is seldom experienced. The listening exercises are challenging. It is so difficult to not interrupt or interject, but it pays huge dividends for communication. The people doing the talking indicate that they felt "heard" or listened to, a type of respect and caring. Those doing the listening often report that once they get past the challenge of not interjecting, it is a type of relief to really hear what is being said.

complete with intellectual bullying by those with higher credentials, or power bullying by those with rank. It is a common feeling that most meetings are not productive; it is obvious that listening and communication are seldom experienced challenging tasks, ones that can impede the progress intended for the meeting.

Leaders who are overwhelmed and preoccupied might find this type of listening to be a challenge. There is overload and frustration with the constant stream of interruptions and conversations. Sometimes it feels like continual chatter in the background. We know from the work of Daniel Goleman how important it is to listen empathically to relate to people in the organization. People want to feel heard, and the gift of listening is one that resonates for the one receiving that gift.

Educational Leaders Who Listen Mindfully

- Listen to hear as opposed to respond, defend, interrupt, argue, or persuade
- Are fully in the moment to be aware and accept what is being said
- Are aware of their own biases that might interfere with mindful listening
- Are attuned with the speaker(s) to demonstrate that what is being communicated is being heard
- Are sensitive and compassionate with the speaker(s), encouraging multiple perspectives instead of dominating or rejecting them
- Are able to listen without judgment, or if a thought of judgment occurs, quickly notes the judgment and returns to hear with compassion

- Will stay with the message, showing patience for the conversations that are challenging
- Will model for others in the school or school district what it means to influence an organization by mindful, patient listening

NONJUDGING

We often judge ourselves by our intentions and others by their actions; if we are intent on school success, seeing how hard we are working, when things fail there can be real confusion. What has happened? Who is at fault? In the stress of needing to produce stronger test results, any failure to achieve may appear to be the result of others in the organization, rather than look for systemic issues.

Leaders are taught to evaluate, supervise, promote, and fire, and they are evaluated on how well they execute these various job descriptions. We live in a world where bottom lines in organizations make headlines. In school districts it is the test performance of students that gets media attention, and leaders are the ones who answer for these scores. *The cycle of judgment might result in blame of others, seeing success as a result of their own actions, and problems the result of others' actions.* It is easy to see how this may occur.

What happens as leaders try and lead while formulating evaluative stances? Judgment often invokes a defensive response—it is a time of fear, discontent, angst, remorse, anger, and other negative emotions. The same is true for others who feel judged within an organization. Currently school leaders are trying to determine and describe valid and reliable measures of learning in their organizations. *Beyond the issue of being evaluated is one of being judged.*

There are numerous situations in which problems are escalated as various groups blame each other for situations in the schools. School leaders may be the subjects of blame as the ones who allowed problems to surface or did not prevent them from happening; as a result they are judged. School leaders are often accused of creating stress in the school and school district when they pass judgment on situations that need attention.

Social and emotional intelligence provides approaches to solving problems that do not rely on judgment for productive solutions; it is all in the way that the communication is delivered. A challenge for administrators is to contemplate their judgments of self and others. Administrators may be trapped in a cycle of projecting blame as a result of complaints that surface, and then absorbing it as stress grows.

The way out of the blame game is to actively channel judgment into an acceptance of *what is*, without criticism and blame. From acceptance, it is possible to look for constructive means of problem resolution. An important distinction for leaders is to be able to provide feedback and information that inspires and motivates.

Educational Leaders Who Mindfully Practice Nonjudgment

- Suspend thoughts of criticism or blame of others
- Suspend thoughts of self-criticism
- Accept what is occurring in the school or school district as a foundation for moving forward and encourage others to feel inspired to work collaboratively
- Demonstrate empathy to build human agency in the district
- Work deliberately to build attunement with people in the school and school district
- Actively listen and observe the teachers, parents, and students for the essential information they yield about the district
- Use influence that is possible with relationship building to encourage growth as opposed to judgment
- Compassionately interact with people within the school and school system to mentor and coach

NONREACTIVITY

Nonreactivity refers to the ability to be with what is happening without over-reacting. Leaders benefit from being able *to respond to as opposed to react to events that are happening.* With critical events happening every day it would be easy for any person of authority to react with anger, sharpness of language, or even sarcasm. There is an expression that goes something like, *"You know why some people are able to push your buttons? It is because they installed them in the first place."* And so it may appear with the people who bring challenges to the leader in the form of criticism, negative comments, or resistance.

It takes patience and acceptance to be in a situation without reacting to it. Obviously, leaders' comments are subject to the review of anyone and everyone in the organization, with commentary and eyewitness rundowns of what occurred, shared with those willing to listen. *A comment can divide, strengthen, or repair relationships.*

Reacting to stressful events can also contribute to a cycle of stress. Something stressful occurs, a defensive posture and reaction follows, resulting in additional stress and a cascading problem. Reactions can become habitual, with the cycle of angst that can raise blood pressure and alienate others.

The alternate to reacting is the response; a quieter form of communication that is possible when the person engaged is fully in the moment without judgment or criticism. It involves the purposeful and peaceful responding to what occurred without anger or overreaction. It also means being able to step away from the emotional hijacking to focus on what really matters. Mindfulness practice helps with building the response to stressful situations.

Educational Leaders Who Practice Mindful Nonreactivity

- Give space between what is heard or witnessed before responding
- Are aware of their own feelings, noting when one topic or issue creates an emotional reaction, using restraint to quell a reaction, waiting for some time and space with which to respond
- Continually remind themselves of the importance of building liaisons, partnerships, and community, as part of their organizational awareness
- Are aware of the cultural complexities that might result in explosive and destructive conversations, modeling responses that are compassionate and empathetic
- Focus on being attuned with the people in the school or school district to actively seek out multiple opinions and interactions
- Are patient for peaceful resolutions to be arranged as opposed to a reaction that results in the loss of partnerships or sense of community
- Commit to the affective dimensions of leadership—believing in the possibility of a compassionate, inclusive, and socially just school and school district
- Are willing to practice stillness and quiet that can increase the possibility of allowing room or space before responding

PATIENCE—*WHEN IT WAS NEEDED YESTERDAY*

How can leaders show patience when their lives are full of urgent demands? School principals feel stress from work, reporting lives that are out of balance with little time to complete tasks at hand, constant interruptions at work, with a loss of joy for the job (Wells et al., 2011). It is challenging to keep up a frantic pace, one where patience is not a primary feeling. The sheer volume of work with little time to complete can leave educational leaders feeling exhausted.

Patience, on the other hand, contributes to a peaceful distance and means of reviewing what is occurring. When leaders listen to truly hear what is being said from employees, it is achieved partly through the intention to be patient and observe. Leaders who demonstrate patience are there for others who have a story or a message to be heard. They can sit with or be with a problem at hand, not rushing impetuously to judgment or an inappropriately timed solution. *Patience yields room for clarity to emerge.*

Leaders who practice patience provide a richness of allowing things to be as they are without trying to manipulate them. Jon Kabat-Zinn (2009) views patience as a type of wisdom. Patience allows instead of forcing, and it gives time and space for things and people to emerge. Interestingly, it takes time to develop patience, particularly if one prizes quick action and immediacy of thought. *Patience yields a different kind of power—a powerful and observant view of what is happening in the moment.*

Patience is a challenge for leaders who feel that they should be the proverbial "point guard" in the world of work, bringing the "ball down the court" and always *doing*, offering solutions, solving problems, and making things happen. It may seem unnatural to wait, to push a pause button, to sit in stillness, to patiently listen. The hurried pace of the educational leader pushes the expectancy and the deadlines of the clock into sharp focus. Mindfulness changes that frantic perspective.

Educational Leaders Who Demonstrate Mindful Patience

- Are willing to accept what is in the moment without demanding immediate action
- Take the time to allow events to unfold without forcing or resisting
- Demonstrate careful attention to listen to what people are saying
- Take inventory of self to manage emotions and self-regulate
- Are attuned to what others are thinking, allowing the relationships to unfold
- Are willing to practice mindfulness to develop patience and compassion
- Demonstrate willingness to entertain thoughts on the full range of emotions for the insights they might yield

TRUST

Trust is vitally important to the success of a leader. Leaders need to feel trust in their own level of ability to perform the job and in their trust of others in the system; they are judged on whether or not they are trusted by others. Goleman, Boyatzis, and McKee (2002) related the importance of trust as one variable when positive groups of people make positive change. Bryk and Schneider (2004) found that relational trust was the one factor that had the greatest power in explaining the success of schools in Chicago over a ten-year period of time. They further found that leaders contributed to the high levels of trust building in the schools.

Kouzes and Posner (2010) related numerous examples of how high-trust organizations outperform counterparts with low trust, indicating that as people generate more trust, the more that others will be willing to do for them. Trust must begin with the leader.

Leaders who are stressed, betrayed, or confronted may not intentionally think about the issue of trust. *They may be thinking of survival.* Fear may surface with the rapid course of change that is happening in their schools or school districts. There are legitimate concerns about what can happen to a leader in a school, as in any organization. People witness, for example, the tenuous nature of superintendents who lose the support when a special interest group surfaces or new members of a school board are elected. These are situations that are played out in the public eye, with recordings, media, and headlines. Educational leaders respond continually to emerging issues, often with little or no warning. It is easy to be blindsided. The same is true for building principals who may fall out of favor after a particular staffing decision, a decision about faculty layoff, or myriad other high-stake decisions.

The word "trust" is often substituted for other words that convey a feeling of community. Goleman (1998) included authenticity with high regard for others and high degrees of integrity as other measures indicative of trust. People often describe a type of intuitive feel about the trust of a leader, a feeling of trust versus distrust. Trust may be a first step in reclaiming a lost relationship. Trust also refers to the beliefs that leaders have in trusting others as opposed to feeling cynical, skeptical, or judgmental of them. *Mindfulness can help with that process.*

Mindfulness practice also refers to the trust that one has in oneself, an element that is often not described in the literature about trust. Self-trust means that the leader has a belief in his or her abilities, which may be challenged as the leader is challenged. Leaders need to believe in and trust their abilities to lead, something that may be compromised in challenging times.

Trusting of oneself includes a basic belief in one's own innate wisdom (Kabat-Zinn, 2009). People who learn to practice mindfulness are taught the importance of following their own innate wisdom. It may take time to cultivate the trust in one's inner wisdom, gained from insights that are propelled by mindfulness practice as the leader looks with compassion at the common humanity of problems that exist in any organization. *Resilience helps to build belief in the self to lead.*

Educational Leaders Who Demonstrate Mindful Trust

- Are willing to be fully present for what is happening in the school or school district to develop insights and innate wisdom as a foundation for trust
- Use compassionate understanding of others to develop relationships and relational trust

- Use stillness to gain an understanding of self-regulation and abilities to develop trust in one's own ability to lead
- Believe in the capacity of others in the school and school district and communicate that belief
- Build trust to build capacity in others to lead and develop potential
- Let go of any feelings that are harshly self-critical to work toward the development of trust in one's own leadership abilities
- Respond to people in the school and school district with a message about the belief that they have the answers to the problems they experience
- Are willing to enter into stillness and mindfulness practice even when the leader would rather do something else—understanding the importance of the discipline of practice

KEY CONCEPTS

- Compassionate leading serves the people in the organization; school leaders who demonstrate compassion are able to detach from judgment and find empathy in action for students, teachers, parents
- Self-compassion is a challenge for educational leaders who *expect perfection in all that they do*; school leadership is difficult and leaders need to *"give themselves a break"* realizing the enormous job they fulfill
- A self-compassionate voice *whispers, "I understand"*—allowing for educational leaders to move forward and stay in their roles as leaders
- Educational leaders learn patience and trust in their abilities to lead when they practice mindfulness with its emphasis on stillness
- Accepting *what is* allows educational leaders to realistically witness what is happening in the school and school district as the foundation for what needs to be completed in the future
- Letting go of past problems, mental or physical clutter, and other ideas or things that no longer matter is a gift offering renewal to an educational leader; *letting go is something that only one can give to him or herself*—no one can do that for another
- The power in listening is *listening to hear*, instead of to interrupt, argue a point, add another point, or dismiss
- Listening to hear can be the greatest gift to someone in a time of need; people want to be listened to
- We often over-listen to people with whom we agree and under-listen to those with whom we disagree
- Mindfulness trains people to listen—to all of the glorious and often "not-heard" communication that fades in the back of a busy and preoccupied world

- Listening adds S-P-A-C-E to a crowded agenda or noisy world
- Nonreactivity allows leaders to be with whatever is happening without reacting to it; the emphasis on observation allows educational leaders to proverbially sit on the bleachers of any event and watch the action on the playing field, without reacting to it
- Nonreactivity teaches leaders a way of responding, one that can build partnerships in times of challenge

Chapter 7

Being Instead of Doing—The Life of a Mindful Leader

WHAT DO I DO WITH THIS STRESS?

A little nick here, a little nick there, and pretty soon you're bleeding to death.

This question is a quiet topic at professional conferences, one that garners attention and empathy. The stress is often raging—it's the hours, the conflict, the negotiations, the test scores, the budgets, the e-mails. The list appears almost infinite. Educational leaders are not alone in handling stress on the jobs. Physician related stress is well documented in the research literature, with 30 percent to 60 percent listed as being in a state of burnout at any time in their career (Dyrbye & Shanafelt, 2011; Krasner et al., 2009).

The burnout rate for educational leaders is absent in the literature; however, there are recent studies that affirm the seriousness of stress for educational leaders (Hawk & Martin, 2011; Wells et al., 2011). Concerns have been raised about the lack of teachers who are willing to enter the profession of school leadership; the attrition rate has many concerned for who will fill the many openings of retirement and career transitions (Fink & Brayman, 2006; Grubb & Flessa, 2006).

Workplace stress contributes to myriad health complaints and trips to a physician; it also contributes to work-related absence and health leaves (Sorenson, 2007). Chronic levels of stress also contribute to problems for leaders whose reasoning and cognition may be impaired as a result (Goleman & Boyatzis, 2008). These authors reported how stress or threat from the leader at work impairs the memory and creativity of the workers.

In fact, anger from bosses, or criticism that is poorly delivered, causes surges in stress hormones in the recipients of that stress. By understanding the social circuitry or social intelligence, leaders may be able to become more adept at reading people and situations and delivering feedback that is compassionate as well as growth producing.

In the same manner that leaders can create stress for people in the organization, leaders can also contribute to the emotional climate in a positive manner. Leaders are able to create a positive tone within the organization. Goleman and Boyatzis (2005) related the characteristics of social intelligence as factors that can be understood to alleviate stress and improve organizational effectiveness of leaders.

Social intelligence factors lend themselves to mindfulness and mindful leadership in several ways. The characteristics of social intelligence are supported by tenets of mindfulness. Table 7.1 lists the various components of social intelligence and shows the parallel of those components with mindfulness.

It is interesting to review how mindfulness and mindful leadership relates to social intelligence, which was informed by advances in neuroscience. Goleman and Boyatzis (2008) related the discoveries of empathy where people attune to others in a type of interconnectedness. These authors posited that it was the social skill sets that leaders develop in others that result in garnering the support and cohesive spirit that is needed for advancing quality.

Table 7.1   Social Intelligence and Mindful Leadership

Social Intelligence	Relation to Mindful Leadership
Empathy—sensitivity to others and their needs	Empathy is central to mindfulness, where a focus is on compassionate understanding
Attunement—Listening to others with attention and thinking about how they feel	Attunement is aligned with the empathetic listening to others
Organizational Awareness—An appreciation of the values and cultures of the organization	Mindfulness practice involves the observation of the present moment, something invaluable to understanding and being aware of the organization
Influence—The ability to persuade others by including them in important discussions and connecting to their interests	Mindfulness is influential with its practice of listening and compassion, traits that can be demonstrated in an organizational setting
Developing others—The coaching and mentoring of others with compassion	Compassion and nonjudgment are central to mindfulness
Inspiration—Articulating a shared vision that builds cohesion and energy	Traits of mindfulness such as compassion, empathy, and nonjudgment contribute to traits that may inspire others
Teamwork—Engaging input from all people in the organization	Mindfulness practice engages others because of the devotion to listening and nonjudgment while being aware and attentive to the present moment.

Source: Wells (2015).

They related the importance of findings of neuroscience in which *the delivery of messages from leaders impacted followers more than the actual content of the message.* Mindful leadership that integrates components of mindfulness and social intelligence may contribute to the success of the leader and the reduction of the stress of the leader.

How Mindfulness Contributes to Stress Reduction

Evidence-based information about the benefits of mindfulness practice is drawn from the over 1,000 reported studies (Ryback, 2009). They emphasize the various health benefits such as increased immunity, positive emotional response, decreased blood pressure, and anxiety that are facilitated by mindfulness practice.

Kabat-Zinn refers to mindfulness as being *simple but not easy.* It may be challenging for school leaders to begin a program of mindfulness practice.

Text Box 7.1

The graduate students in my class are what I refer to as "full-time everything" as workers, students, committed family members, etc. They are basically sleep-deprived people, attending graduate school in the evening after working a full day. And they are attending school events on nights when they are not taking classes, leaving little time for anything for them. In a Human Resource class that I teach, we develop an individual wellness plan that is research based, one that they choose and enact for a period of six weeks. They choose anything from physical exercise, mindfulness practice, Hatha yoga, or another program of their choosing. The majority of the students choose yoga or mindfulness. Initially there is disbelief that there is time to conduct a self-study, but the assignment aspect makes it an *intention.* Afterward, the students report a feeling of tremendous relief from stress with the unique experience of doing something just for them. We then apply all of the learning to how a district might offer a wellness program to its employees. Even with a six-week wellness program with a practice time allotment chosen by the student, the enthusiasm and appreciation are incredible. Virtually every student reports stress relief and a sense of appreciation for what is possible. Students used to come to class with some pride in being able to "multitask." Now there seems to be a growing consensus that this type of life is like a drain of joy in a system that is overwhelming and unrelenting. Mindfulness practice reinforces the neuroscience data, which documents that multitasking is a myth and mindfulness allows for a *presence* that offers the *present* of calm.

There can be many reasons for this: lack of time, exhaustion, frustration, lack of knowledge of its efficacy, or discipline to practice when everything else needs immediate attention. The list of expectations and requirements is extensive for school leaders. Mindfulness is a discipline of practice.

With the busyness of work, school leaders may need to intentionally give themselves permission to watch their children play a sport, go to a movie, delight in a dinner out with friends, walk barefoot in the grass, exercise, anything that is not dictated by official agenda. We have become a nation of people not making use of vacations, or going on vacation from work, but not really leaving it by checking e-mails throughout the day.

There probably isn't a day that goes by where there isn't a headline or story in the media about stress and stress-related problems. Educational leaders become accustomed to acute and chronic levels of stress, with a danger of thinking that chronic stress is somehow natural. Mindfulness offers a different approach to dealing with stress.

Mindfulness allows for people to be in stillness, and experience the quiet of the moment. In sitting in stillness, it is possible to be aware of thoughts as they appear. Rather than striving to somehow deny or "wrestle the stress to the ground," it is possible to pause the continual *doing* mode and just *be*. In other words, it is possible to feel and observe what is occurring, and take some moments to sit with it, or be with it, without trying to control it.

Educational Leaders Who Mindfully Deal with Stress Reduction

- Have a distinct benefit of *knowing what to do when the going gets rough*
- Are able to help others in the school or school district to find sources of stress reduction
- Are able to listen to situations in the school with a calm perspective
- Are more likely to find a path of self-compassion
- Are likely to show empathy to others needing supportive guidance
- Have learned the benefits of seeking stillness in times of stress
- Understand the value of giving permission to slow down the administrative world and create healthy boundaries
- Serve as a model of influence for learning how to thrive instead of merely coping in stressful situations
- Take the time needed to be in the moment with a calm perspective
- Are aware when their emotions are beginning to react instead of respond to situations
- Are likely to have learned about the need for patience with learning how to find peace and calm, as well as the natural feelings of sadness or regret

POLITICAL REALITY—ENDING THE SLIDE FROM BAD TO HORRIBLE

Educational leaders live in a type of glass house where all the windows are open; virtually all actions, communications, and discussions become grist for the mill. Things can go upside down in a moment's notice, and when it is least expected. The political reality is not always apparent, and it is challenging to know where the political currency is at any given moment.

Heifetz and Linsky (2002) described the political reality of leaders who might feel invulnerable, not sizing up the landscape for what is occurring in the moment. They advocated for understanding those who are on board with the movement in the organization, those who oppose, and those in the middle. By paying attention to each group, a leader is able to continue to size up the political atmosphere and respond accordingly.

Heifetz and Linsky (2002) suggested that it is first and foremost important to build relationships with people in the organization, a common thread in the literature on leadership. They reported, "The lone warrior myth of leadership is a sure route to heroic suicide" (p. 100). They further explained the importance of keeping the opposition close to understand their perspectives and continue to work with them.

The common denominator in this message is the successful navigation of working with people and relationship building, all helped by the qualities of emotional and social intelligence where leaders can self-regulate, demonstrate empathy, and develop and influence others. Mindfulness for leaders places importance on these traits, all cultivated by the constructs of mindfulness meditation, such as awareness, acceptance, compassion, listening, patience, trust, and being fully present.

HOW MINDFULNESS PRACTICE CULTIVATES STRENGTHS IMPORTANT FOR DEALING WITH THE POLITICAL REALITY

Mindfulness practice cultivates the strengths that are important to understanding how to respond to and develop a different way of being in the organization. The repetitive prompts of mindfulness practice focus on emotional and social intelligence where leaders stop and *listen to hear, learn to not judge, learn patience, develop spaciousness around problems and issues, become truly aware of what is happening in the moment, accept what is happening instead of denying or avoiding it, develop compassionate understanding, generate self-compassion for their own shortcomings or missteps, and importantly learn to let go of things that are in the past or those that cannot be changed.*

These shifts in reality are not automatic; they rely on practice. Our minds take us relentlessly back to our default settings where we listen to our own opinions over and over again, judge others who fail to meet our expectations, become impatient with results that are not fast or *right* enough, feel the clutter of the problems and the ambiguity of those problems, see a different version of reality rather than what is truly happening in the moment, refuse to accept the reality of what is happening in the moment, feel angry at self or others who have brought problems into the organization, or hold fast on to the former communications or problems that have been indelibly cast in the past and played over and over in the present. Does this sound at all familiar? Most people will recognize themselves in some of these default mechanisms.

Richie Davidson (2012), an affective neuroscientist, provided insights for leaders who want to change their default or automatic patterns of thinking. He stated:

> But we now know that this picture of a static, unchanging brain is wrong. Instead, the brain has a property called neuroplasticity, the ability to change its structure and function in significant ways. The change can come about in response to the experiences we have as well as the thoughts we think. (p. 9)

Davidson advocated for the role of mindfulness meditation in cultivating changes in neuroplasticity of the brain.

Mindfulness practice offers a release from the default reactions in the mind. It is not an overnight process, but it is possible by a gentle reminder of the importance of listening, accepting reality, developing compassion for self and others, with the intention of letting go of issues and problems from the past. These qualities are strengthened by the continual deep and gentle plunge into stillness where the focus and the intention are on the present moment, all without judgment of self or others. With time, the practice becomes more easily evident in the present, and when it isn't, a voice in the head might offer a reminder such as: **"Think patience, see compassion, listen to hear, accept what is happening and just *be* with it, let go of the struggles of the past or the worry of tomorrow, trust yourself that you can practice *being* over *doing*, and see this freshly with beginner's eyes."** With practice, there is a different perspective, one that is inclusive and trusting of self and others.

Educational Leaders Who Mindfully Practice Attending to the Political Reality

- Are fully present to be aware of what is happening in the school or school district, reducing their distraction and preoccupation

- Listen to what is being said and otherwise communicated by the people in the system, taking care to not over-listen to the areas of agreement and under-listen to areas of disagreement
- Practice patience with people in the school and school district to build relationships that serve them well in times of stress
- Develop others to be part of the team that is moving forward with the district vision
- Inspire others to grow and contribute in the schools and school district
- Believe in the people in the school district for their capacity to make a difference
- Attune with all groups within the schools and school district, regardless of ideology of interest group
- Respond to issues as they emerge—paying attention to the wake-up calls
- Show compassion for people who are encountering difficulties within the system
- Actively recruit people who have been marginalized or discounted in the past within the system for the contributions they will make, and for the leaders' belief in and commitment to inclusion and social justice

GETTING TO WE INSTEAD OF ME

Leaders do not lead alone; they are involved with a whole cast of people in the organization whose positions are interdependent to the success of the business at hand. Educational leaders who cultivate a sense of "we" are the ones who can build capacity among the employees to believe that they make a difference. Workplace accomplishments are the result of people working as teams to create a difference. Transformation is not a solo act; it is the result of people supporting the major efforts in the organization. Getting to the "we" in an organization is not automatic—it takes leadership to build the foundation and support for becoming a team.

To build capacity within an organization, to form a team, or to build for "we" instead of "me" is an art form. The practices of mindfulness can be viewed as common denominators for building capacity in an organization. Specifically, the *constructs of listening and compassion set the foundation for being attentive, aware, and accepting.* People, who are mindful, accept what is there in the present as opposed to denying, rejecting, hiding from, or looking away. When this occurs, people are open to reality. The formation of a team necessitates a focus on the reality of a situation.

Educational leaders who are patient listeners, ones who are nonjudgmental and empathic, have an advantage in building relationships among the staff. It takes patience and trust to build the capacity within an organization to bring others on board with a vision for forward movement. But without that relational trust, others will not be fully invested in that vision. Leaders have described that the process of getting to "we" is like *walking a tightrope on a windy day*, one in which any problem can upset the balance and forward movement. *It often takes going back to qualities such as compassion, listening, nonjudgment, and acceptance to remind others that they matter. These qualities are built by practice; it is how leaders evolve, change, and grow.*

Educational Leaders Who Mindfully Practice Getting to We

- Attune with others to bring them on board with others in the district
- Build relationships with others in the district
- Show empathy for those who are estranged from the forward movement in the district
- Practice, in earnest, efforts to develop and coach others
- Believe in the importance of the teachers and parents to advocate on behalf of the students
- Respond to the issues that the constituents bring forward in the district
- Let go of past regrets and limiting thoughts that limit collaboration
- Listen to people in the organization with respect and interest
- Resolve to serve instead of force
- Practice self-regulation to continually monitor behavior
- Articulate a vision for building a sense of community within the school or school district

LIFE AFTER BURNOUT

Leaders who give of themselves to a point of exhaustion may face burnout, which typically includes cynicism, hopelessness, and feelings of inefficiency (Maslach & Leiter, 2008). Burnout is something that might be difficult for leaders to admit, because of the need to project the forward motion expected of leadership, the ego, and a sense of vulnerability with such disclosure.

For educational leaders, burnout can be even more challenging because of the work that they do on behalf of students; it can be very difficult, for example, to admit depersonalization with regard to thinking about students or teachers in need. *Emotional exhaustion leaves leaders in a tough place.*

Heifetz and Linsky (2002) described the dangers inherent in leading, particularly when leaders are initiating changes that require more substantial reworking of attitudes and working habits. They described the problems that ensued when people they did not anticipate as resisting their efforts, did indeed resist. Boyatzis and McKee (2005) referred to sacrifice syndrome as the cycle in which leaders often find themselves, the result from giving so much on the job and experiencing chronic and acute levels of stress. Interestingly, these authors related compassion as an important means of dealing with the most challenging issues.

Heifetz and Linsky (2002) suggested that leaders should listen actively, and accept new ideas that are different than their own. They also suggested being curious because the solutions do not happen overnight after a crisis, with a reminder that resisters are also right at times. They related the importance of building strong relationships to bolster them in the most difficult times, being able to facilitate conflict so that opposing views can surface. They advocated for leaders to remove themselves from the dance floor of the action and gain perspective from an elevated place, one they refer to as the balcony, a place where they can see with greater clarity and interpret what is happening.

Boyatzis and McKee (2005) called for hope, compassion, and mindfulness as necessary components of renewal. They viewed mindfulness not as the meditative state, but as being *aware, awake, and attentive.* They saw these actions as part of intentional change where leaders would take deliberate steps to define and renew the self. They advocated building emotional and social intelligence to build capacity in themselves and others.

Mindfulness practice would help with renewal of leaders by encouraging leaders to be fully present, in the moment, actively listening without judging, displaying a sense of hope and compassion within the organization. Renewal can be a challenging concept for a leader dealing with emotional exhaustion. The first thought might be to get away for a vacation, a complete break from the actual workplace, be it the school or school district.

However, the workplace is often taken along in the suitcase, briefcase, or purse as leaders check in throughout the day and evening for messages, texts, voice-mail, and e-mail. They are not *really away from it all.* Then, when they

Text Box 7.2

The issue of conflict is an interesting one to consider. Most people would prefer to avoid it—that is understood. However, there are other considerations of conflict. One metaphor that has some reference for leaders is taken from sailing. There is basically only one condition under which sailors cannot sail. I pose this question in classes. Unless someone has a history of sailing, the question usually goes unanswered. The one condition is the absence of wind! Sailors can sail in rough seas—they adjust their sails. The weather might be rough, and they might be in the middle of white water, and yet by adjusting the sails they can move through it. Mindfulness offers us similar options. When the water of our experience is rough, mindfulness allows us to adjust the sails and move through the problems.

physically return to the workplace, there is the *"reentry phase"* where it often feels like merging with traffic on a crowded highway. Reentry can make it feel like one never got away in the first place. How does mindfulness help with renewal and reentry?

How Mindfulness Helps with Renewal After Burnout

Mindfulness allows leaders to live in the moment, and that would mean fully accepting the reality of any emotion, be it sadness, grief, joy, or elation. As leaders sit with the challenges that they face, they are acknowledging their feelings and facing them, without criticism, and with compassion for themselves and others. The practice cultivates patience and an ability to react as opposed to responding. These attributes are important leadership qualities, and they help with life after burnout.

Denying or resisting the reality of the situation does not help burnout. Ask anyone who is resisting anything, *"How is that working for you?"* and you will receive an answer something like, *"It's not."* To resist often means that someone avoids what is happening, prolonging the agony, in this case, the burnout. There is wisdom in the saying, *"The only way through it is through it."* In this case, mindfulness allows the process of going through it, by *facing it, sitting with it, and accepting the reality of it.*

So, what may seem counterintuitive, such as the being, the sitting, the listening, the accepting, the nonjudgment, the compassion, and the letting go, are part of the way through, to a quiet healing and restoration. *Mindful leadership whispers in a way that is felt, not shouted.*

Davidson (2011) offered a statement at a scientific conference that has direct application, and a beacon of hope for educational leaders whose lives are touched by profound levels of stress, and who make a decision to work with mindfulness meditation as a disciplined practice. He stated,

> One of the themes that you'll be hearing repeatedly over the next two and a half days is the idea that there are certain positive qualities, such as happiness and compassion, that the contemplative traditions teach us are not fixed characteristics. We are not indelibly fixed in our current state, but rather these are characteristics that can be transformed. There is a very precious and important convergence of that idea with the modern concept of neuroplasticity—that the brain can change in response to experience and training—a convergence that provides a foundation for us as scientists to go forward in a truly novel and integrative way. (pp. 23–24)

Davidson's research provides leaders with the thought that there is learning in meditative practice, and that the practice can provide resilience and hope for educational leaders, something that might otherwise have led to a

Text Box 7.3

Mindfulness helps people to refresh and renew while one the job, in any moment. All it takes is the intention to be fully present, to allow the breath to go to work in a restorative way. Each new breath is a fresh beginning, and each exhale is a complete letting go of the past, yesterday, or the last ten minutes. The rhythm of the natural breath can gently soothe. When people are upset or in stress, the breathing is often shallow and terse. Slowing the pace of that experience to be fully present in the moment is to allow for a relaxed breathing to occur. It may take three or four breaths with eyes closed and an intentional focus on the breath as it enters the nostrils and leaves the lungs. Let it be a source of peace, the portable anchor that is always available. Just stay with it when you want to leave, run, or be elsewhere. Staying with the breath can prove to be a blessing, one that restores a sense of balance and importantly, allows you to stay with what is occurring. Let the rhythm of the breath carefully and gently take care of you, in this moment, this breath, this moment. We learn that it is not about escaping, it is the process of *being with* that allows people to stay the course and renew while being on the job. This is one of the biggest gifts for an exhausted school leader to consider. *And, the good news is that it is possible to renew, with self-compassion, without judgment, and with a practice of learning to be in the moment with the breath.*

job change or retirement. Meditation provides an opportunity for staying the course, staying in the game, and thriving. It seems that something that provides stress relief may also improve practice. It is the intentional pairing of mindfulness practice, with social and emotional intelligence, resonant leadership, and scientific findings from neuroscience that combine to conceptualize mindfulness for educational leaders.

Learning how to push the pause button and gently breathe can be a constant source of help as school leaders learn to bounce back after burnout; these are qualities that help throughout the day, in the moment of stress or upset.

Educational Leaders Who Are Mindfully Thriving After Burnout

- Have learned that resilience is possible after a personal or professional crisis
- Develop trust in their ability to use mindfulness to work through problems
- Learn that resistance to the problems does not lead to their resolution
- Are poised to help others learn the same
- Can influence the development of aspiring and practicing leaders to stay the course

- Learn the importance of being fully present to be able to observe, sense, and notice what is happening in the school and school district
- Learn the importance of self-compassion in moving forward
- *Know that there is life after cynicism, feelings of inefficiency, or depersonalization*

REALLY LIVING IN THE MOMENT

The concept of living in the moment is a challenging one. We live in many time zones throughout the day, *usually the past or the future tense.* The moments of the past might be one that are replayed throughout the day, thoughts of regret or anger at self or others. The past has a rather sneaky way of arriving and intruding in the most serene of moments, bringing someone back to a time that is replayed in the mind over and over again. Then there is the tomorrow of the mind, that time of anticipation, often with concern or worry of what tomorrow's agenda includes. Many people reside in the future tense; always trying to anticipate what is next, juggling what is half-done with what needs to be done. It can be challenging to escape this future orientation. *The mind can be an endless list of things that needs attention.* The headlines are full of stories of people who feel that they need to be everywhere. People's to-do lists are never finished.

The point of living in the moment escapes most people, a comment that is generated when people begin practicing mindfulness. The practice of

Text Box 7.4

Talk about burnout is often raised in class as a question or pondering, "I wonder if I am getting burned out?" or "I think the people in our school are burned out." The class can become a place of safety where the colleagues in the cohort offer a sense of loyalty and concern for others. These types of questions also generate a cascade of emotions, with people expressing similar feelings. Within minutes of discussion, there is often a general consensus that being burned out is rather commonplace among educational leaders. The leaders in the classes often describe feeling like they are on the edge of coping, with fatigue as a primary emotion, or they ascribe similar emotions to leaders they observe. They did not expect to have the degree of problems when they signed on for the job, and the problems often seem to have no end. The feelings, in general are about not having enough hours in the day to complete the work that is expected, with some resignation that this is how the world of educational leadership operates.

Text Box 7.5

Many times leaders in my leadership classes speak of getting through the day, week, or year; there is widespread agreement in terms like *enduring or surviving* the year or a board meeting, negotiations, media interviews. As I listen to the stories of people describing crises in their schools or school districts, I hear a type of what I would refer to as *resignation* that this is the way it is, in the situation. Aspiring leaders often nod their heads as the stories are told of what happens in their school or district, often sharing things they have witnessed. The personal narratives are quite compelling. There is often restlessness as the stories unfold. Some aspiring leaders say that they are not sure if they want to lead; others question their ability to lead with the challenges that are waiting for them, should they decide to take a position as a leader.

mindfulness helps people to realize that they are often in the past or the future with the thinking process; the present tense is elusive.

Educational Leaders Who Are Mindfully Living in the Moment

- Have learned the importance of being fully present in the moment
- Are able to accept *what is* as opposed to *what was* or *will be*
- Have an advantage of most likely knowing what is happening in the school or district as opposed to being preoccupied or distracted
- Can listen to the people in the school or district with the integrity of being fully present for them, foundational to influencing others
- Can respond to issues as they emerge

LEADING WITH OTHERS AS LEADERS

Educational leaders do not lead in isolation; they lead with a whole array of people who provide vision, support, and imagination to fuel the efforts in the organization. A parallel to understanding the unique distribution of roles and responsibilities of leadership can be witnessed in the world of sports; people understand the importance of team effort in any contest. Defense and offense work together; there are coaches and managers, people who sit on the bench and those who start the game. Everyone plays an important role.

In schools, superintendents are key to forming the team that works collaboratively to make things happen in the district. Leadership is broadly distributed among central office personnel, building level administrators, and teacher leaders. If leaders are involved with building capacity for others to lead, the constructs of mindfulness that are listed in this book, including patience, trust, listening, awareness, attending, compassion, nonjudgment, nonreactivity, and acceptance, can provide qualities that are aligned with leadership that invites and nurtures leadership among others. The issue of trust receives prominence in the literature about leadership.

Palmer (2004) commented on the circle of trust among people that is without an agenda, where "we practice the paradox of being alone together, of being present to one another as a community of solitudes" (p. 54). Palmer referred to the ways in which solitude and community work together, much like the ways in which mindfulness practice introduces the solitude of the individual embedded in the context of community.

Leadership with others embraces a strong sense of community, and mindfulness qualities support the development of community. As schools continue to become places of shared leadership, where leaders cultivate the capacity of all to lead, there is a new sense of community that can be bolstered by the practice of mindfulness.

How the Practice of Mindfulness Contributes to Leading with Others

Mindfulness practice, by the qualities that it encourages, may contribute to the interest in a shared leadership. Practicing mindfulness allows leaders to hit the pause button and listen to others whose opinions may otherwise be overlooked or ignored. The acts of nonreactivity and nonjudgment contribute to the inclusion of others as leaders because they are seen with fresh eyes instead of judging eyes; these actions, by their sense of being, invite participation.

Goleman (2000) referred to the emotional and social intelligence of leaders, making *the hard case for soft skills* in which leaders develop emotional awareness, trustworthiness, and empathy to serve and lead in their organizations. Mindfulness practice encourages the cultivation of emotional and social intelligence, qualities that invite and attract others to participate as leaders.

Educational Leaders Who Practice Mindfully Leading with Others as Leaders

- Attune with others in the schools and school district
- Listen to what is being communicated within the district for purposes of bringing others on board as leaders

- Believe in the capacity of others to lead, and cultivate their leadership presence
- Respond to issues that may divide faculty or staff
- Know what the culture of the organization is to bring aboard others as leaders
- Inspire and influence others to join in the vision to contribute to the leadership of the school and school district
- Develop others as leaders in the school and school district

WHEN THINGS *ARE* WORKING

Consider the following description for an educational leader, assuming that the requisite technical skills and degrees are earned. *Wanted—a leader for our school/school district who possesses the following traits:*

Compassionate, nonjudgmental, good listener, capable of being fully present in all situations whether good or challenging, demonstrating trust, patience, and acceptance.

This is a job description of mindfulness traits that are developed through mindfulness practice, demonstrating how mindfulness is both a state and a trait (Smalley & Winston, 2010). Since research has already shown that most managers have the threshold technical expectations for a job, it is the connection with people that ultimately makes a difference in effective levels (Boyatzis & McKee, 2005; Goleman, 2000).

Text Box 7.6

While graduate students in educational leadership classes bring issues and concerns to class to gain perspective and seek different or more effective solutions to the problems they see in their schools and school districts, they are also quick to point out when things are working and when there is a sense of community or belonging for moving forward. These aspiring and practicing leaders' comments align with research provided by Goleman (2000) that explained how emotional intelligence made a profound difference in leading, over traditional intelligence measures or IQ. When these graduate students talk about what is working within their schools, they describe leaders whose attributes are ones that attract others to their vision, their requests, or their collaboration. They also describe leaders who have attributes of servant leadership, where they are concerned for the welfare of others and demonstrate that caring for the workers (Greenleaf, 1977).

Educational Leaders Who Practice Mindfulness When Things Are Working

- Know the value of practice—the discipline and peace of entering into stillness
- Give permission for self-care
- Model the way of contemplative practice
- Stay focused of the present moment
- Know the importance of patience—*it takes patience to practice when there are so many other things to do*
- Bring spaciousness to the fleeting moments of the day

KEY CONCEPTS

- Educational leaders who are empathic, attuned with people in the schools, and dedicated to building capacity and teamwork help to reduce stress in the schools and school district
- Stress levels in schools might be chronic—mindfulness teaches a way to not react to it
- Mindfulness teaches how to develop room or spaciousness around problems
- The brain changes with our thoughts and experiences; mindfulness helps to change the default thinking of the brain
- There is life after burnout—something that mindfulness can help educational leaders realize—resilience is built after crisis
- Living in the moment means letting go of the past, and not worrying about tomorrow
- Daniel Goleman's statement, "The hard case for soft skills" represents the learning that is possible with mindfulness as educational leaders focus with intention on being compassionate and nonjudgmental
- Educational leaders who practice mindfulness are living a gift of self-care

Part III

POSSIBILITIES OF MINDFUL LEADERSHIP

Chapter 8

Making Time, Not Finding Time

IT'S THE PRACTICE...

The phrase "Going to practice" has an enticing ring to it; people might imagine going to hit some golf balls, practice or train for a marathon, practice hitting or catching a ball in preparation for softball, working at the practice barre for ballet; the list is endless, depending on one's orientation to practice. The point is that practice in this framework is typically associated with a choice that one pursues.

The practice of mindfulness is similar. It involves choice. It offers something—stillness. Like the practice of sports, it is a discipline. And, in the case of mindful leadership, the practice of mindfulness is linked with mindful leadership traits. It all gets back to practice. The fidelity is to the practice; there is wisdom to be found in the stillness, with *profound insights and healing heard through the whispers of mindfulness practice*. The practice can refer to what happens as people sit in stillness as in meditation. The reference is to practice, as to *engage*. In this case, practice is a verb. There is also the reference to *mindful* leadership practice where mindful is an adjective, or as a noun as in *be mindful*, or as an adverb, such as the art of leading *mindfully*. Leading mindfully includes constructs such as awareness, acceptance, being fully present, compassion, listening, patience, and trust are the way that the leader presents on the job, and influences the culture of the organization. The mindfulness constructs are cultivated from practicing mindful meditation, and reinforced through practice on the job.

For busy leaders, the challenge is time. Many leaders describe time as the enemy—not enough of it, too crammed with endless requests and responsibilities, and out of control. Media headlines are full of stories of people who can't fall asleep at night, those who wake up around 3:00 a.m., or those who wake up well before the alarm sounds. We seem to have a fair amount of sleep-deprived people in our organizations. When at work, many people think of how tired they are, longing to be in bed, sleeping; and at night, many are wide awake with the thoughts of what did not get accomplished during the day, or what the next day will bring. With an unrelenting schedule it is a challenge to first think of time for practice, and also to consider if the practice will lead to something, such as personal or professional benefits.

Mindfulness practice can seem misplaced, such as *"Why am I practicing mindfulness when there are so many important things to do?"* It can also seem boring as in *"Sitting here for a half hour, just watching my breath is boring. I should be doing something."* Mindfulness practice can also appear selfish as in *"Why am I sitting in silence? My kids need clean clothes, the garden needs weeding, I haven't folded the laundry, I have to grade papers, write a report"* or whatever else is on the "to-do" list. The agreement to practice mindfulness is one that involves repetition and discipline, over and over, again and again; Jon Kabat-Zinn often says, *"As if your life depended on it. Because it does."*

> For busy leaders, it is not about finding time; there is no time. It's about making time. It's not about wanting to sit in stillness; it's about just practicing mindfulness, whether it is convenient or not, wanted or not, exciting or not, or interesting or not. It is a habit of disciplined practice.

Exercisers seem to gravitate to the concept of practice, because that is part of their routine, a habit. Likewise, people who practice yoga often relate to the practice of breathing and being in the moment because their yoga practice has reinforced similar concepts. The sticking point for the aspiring and practicing leaders in my graduate education leadership classes seems to be twofold: *How to practice mindfulness, and how to make the time for it.* These are the questions that each person must resolve.

The practice of mindfulness meditation is clearly an investment in time that allows one to work more efficiently, and listen and think more clearly. Preoccupation and distraction are reduced with a more focused attention to the present. Mindfulness meditation helps with stress reduction, which may contribute to ease in resting, calming down, and sleeping. Mindfulness practice pays dividends for educational leaders who may be struggling with chronic levels of stress.

How Mindfulness Reinforces Practice

Practicing anything with regularity helps to create a habit. With mindfulness practice, it can be easy to slip into the busyness of each day by running from

Text Box 8.1

Mindfulness practice is, for most of the graduate students in my classes, reinforcing. Because we have several practices per month with a weekly class, students describe their growth over the term, indicating things such as the difficulty they had in the beginning, just being able to even hear what I was saying during the practice. Their minds were loaded with ideas, full of distracted thoughts. The more we practiced, the more ability they related about being able to settle in to the moment. The students told me that the guided practice from the beginning of the term that became sitting in stillness, toward the end, signaled their ability to quickly enter the present moment without as much guided direction. The silence became the soothing element, not the distraction.

one event or activity to another without catching a breath. Each person must find the path to cultivate regular practice. For some, it could be in the morning before the busy day begins; others might find solace in centering with stillness before falling asleep. A mindful moment can do much to increase the peace of a situation.

Educational Leaders Who Practice Mindfulness

- Increase their chances for lowered anxiety, blood pressure, or depression while increasing the immune response and optimism (Brown & Ryan, 2003; Carmody & Baer, 2007; Greeson, 2009)
- Build the elements of social and emotional intelligence with emphasis on compassion, empathy, trust, patience, acceptance, and listening that mindfulness builds
- Increase their likelihood for staying in their position with a sense of thriving because of the correlation with resilience and positive outlook

THERE'S ALWAYS ONLY NOW

The concept of, "There's always only now" is another liberating reality for the world of a busy leader. It begins a process of stopping the endless time continuum to be fully present for what is happening. It means being there for the conversation that is occurring, observing what is currently happening in the organization, sitting with a disappointment, accepting what is the reality of a situation, or being aware of the meal you are eating. It means bringing back the chatter of the mind to be in the present, instead of a preoccupied future or a regretful past.

Because leaders must constantly juggle the ever-changing present moment, the concept of now might seem to be challenging. If leaders are struggling with being aware of the here and now because of being preoccupied with what is waiting in the front office, the computer e-mail, the next meeting with a parent, student, or teacher, it may seem impossible to settle in one time reality—the present.

In the middle of a chaotic schedule, it might serve a leader to stop and take a deep breath, with a reminder to pause and enter into stillness of thought. A leader could also repeat some phrases to bring the reality of the present moment to the forefront. A new breath is a fresh beginning and the exhalation of that breath is the complete letting go, all within the confines of the present moment.

Educational Leaders Who Mindfully Demonstrate "There's Always Only Now"

- Bring the distracted and preoccupied thoughts back to the present moment—they are fully present for what is happening
- Resist the default of worrying about tomorrow's agenda or yesterday's regrets
- Work with the focus to stay alert—the intention is to be there for people in the school and school district
- Have the tendency to be fully present to actually *listen to hear*, as opposed to answer, with the focus on what is in front of them
- Experience all that comes to the door of the present moment in full attention
- Demonstrate to others that their presence has the leader's full attention
- Model that it is possible to stay present
- Resist the urge to check the cell phone during a conversation or meal with another person
- Don't put the cell phone down in front of them at every meeting, meal, or conversation
- Practice doing what they are doing—watching the pep assembly while watching the pep assembly, for example, instead of using it as a backdrop while mentally traveling to another challenge such as tomorrow's agenda
- Bring the mental wanderings back to the present moment when aware of the wandering

MINDFUL MOMENTS

Mindful moments are the endless possibilities for practice of being in the present moment day or night. They include a willingness to choose an activity that is done routinely or automatically and to engage in that activity with attention, awareness, and intention. Mindful moments can be the ultimate pause button where a leader stops what is happening and fully engages in that moment.

Busy leaders often worry about regular practice because of the pressing time elements. Mindful moments allow for a different type of practice. Rather than engaging in stillness for fifteen minutes, a half hour, or longer, mindful moments are just that—moments, fast and yet deeply healing.

Examples of a mindful moment include taking an ordinary activity such as washing one's hands, sipping a cup of coffee or tea, riding in an elevator, walking up the stairs, taking a shower or bath, washing the dishes, sitting in the garden, or any other activity that can be fully embraced for its own moment. A mindful moment can be restorative and calming in the middle of a day.

People fill their days with mindless, automatic activities: eating, driving, walking, showering; the list is virtually endless. Any one of these activities is an incredible experience. Think for example of the ingenious invention of a hot morning shower, one that is totally lost if the person is fretting over the first meeting of the day, the hostile neighbor, the empty gas tank, or another of the endless possibilities that can interrupt the quiet of a bath or shower.

The same is true for driving; headlines about distracted driving are frequently in the media. People often describe the frantic start to every morning, possibly eating while standing, often rushing to work or school. By making time for, instead of finding time for mindful moments, people can find some calm and create some space in a cluttered, digital world that is in overdrive.

Text Box 8.2

One example of automatic activity is hand washing. Often the hand washing is done while thinking of an impending agenda, or the urgency of what is waiting to be accomplished. People often wash hands throughout the day as they do other activities, fast and without thought, just the push to get on to the next thing at hand. Hand washing can be a time for mindfulness, giving full attention to the act of washing the hands in warm water. It can be the pause in the day, throughout the day. Instead of rushing through the activity, it can be completed slowly, just noticing what is happening.

A mindful washing of the hands would include the feel of the soap, noticing if it is foamy or another substance, noting the water, it if is warm, or cold, or a fast or forceful stream. By mindfully washing the hands, it is possible to stop the rush of the day and be totally in the moment of the activity. Mindful moments can interrupt the distracted preoccupation and frantic pace of the usual *"24/7" connectivity* by allowing space and quiet throughout the day.

The tendency for leaders to pause throughout the day is rare; the race begins before the leader walks into the door and continues throughout the event-jammed day, and it is the moments that can be restorative. Educational leaders report parents waiting for them outside their office well before the start of school; the same is true for requests for evening meetings, text, or e-mail messages. A mindful moment can make the difference in setting a "restart" button in the day of a busy leader, a chance to slow down the pace, and control what might seem like an out-of-control schedule, *even if only for a moment.*

How Mindfulness Contributes to Finding Mindful Moments

Mindfulness practice focuses on the present moment, reinforcing over and over again that it is the "now" that is being recognized. Mindfulness practice teaches people to bring the mind back to the present moment when it wanders off in a different direction. Through the discipline of practice, the mind is brought back to the present, observing what is occurring in breath, thought, hearing, walking, or whatever is the focus of the practice. People learn to witness the moment through this process.

When the day brings its challenges, conversations, meetings, agendas, lunches, and busyness, there is a pause that is always available, and that involves a mindful moment. Leaders may argue that their lack of privacy does not include a space for a mindful moment, and that is where they may need to be resourceful and creative.

With a private office, a phrase can be arranged with an administrative assistant that is simply as easy as *"I need to have some time for myself. I will be right back."* Then, turning the chair to the wall and out of view, the leader can sit in stillness, a time for quiet without phone or human interruption, no checking texts or e-mails, or otherwise working in the office. This mindful pause can last for one to two minutes, with the school leader focusing on the breath and finding stillness within the school day. The breath is portable, always available, and ready to be used in mindfulness practice.

Leaders can also find one to two minutes in the office or classroom after others have left for the day, or just sit in the car before leaving for home. It is not necessary to sit for long periods of time to experience the benefits of mindfulness practice; it can be accomplished "on the fly" as leaders work throughout the day.

Being able to leave the confines of a building is also a means for integrating mindful moments in the day; leaders can leave the building for a brief mindful walk to their car in the parking lot, just focusing on the present moment. The stairs in a building can also be a place for quiet, mindful walking. In a school there is a possibility of going into the halls once the classes are is session, or finding a conference room that is empty. It takes creativity and determination to give oneself *permission* to hit the pause button during the day. It is the mindful moments that can be transformative during the day, offering leaders a "time out" without loss of productivity; in fact, a mindful pause might increase energy by giving a boost to the leader.

Educational Leaders Who Practice Mindful Moments

- Give themselves permission to hit the "pause button" during the workday
- Take time to experience the extraordinary in the ordinary, experiences such as hand washing, sipping a cup of coffee or tea, or the morning shower
- Experience the benefits of slowing down the pace of the day
- Have the opportunity to interrupt stress and experience calm
- Practice listening to the stillness of the moment
- Develop practice with the patience that it takes to slow the frantic world of leading
- Let go of preoccupation and distraction
- Experience the value of self-care throughout the day

FINDING THE CALM IN THE MIDDLE OF THE STORM

Finding the calm in the middle of the storm might seem impossible during the heat of whatever is happening. Problems in schools may be experienced or witnessed in grade levels, departments, administrative ranks, or school districts. There is no shortage of problems or personal encounters that result in tension, crisis, or hurt or angry feelings. People seem to understand that problems exist, and yet approaching these problems to resolve them can be highly challenging. Within a school or school district there is the organizational culture, with endless possibilities for issues and challenges. The culture might include one or two people who disrupt meetings on a regular basis, the history of people who have felt wronged or disregarded, or the problems associated with mishearing, misquoting, misunderstanding, or misapplying what has been heard, as examples.

What is the response to the issues like the ones presented above? How do people cut through the difficult emotions throughout each day and find a sense of calm rather than be lost in another struggle? The answer can be found in a way of *being* as opposed to a way of *doing*—one of the many paradoxes of mindfulness practice and mindful leadership.

Mindful leadership provides a way to face the challenges and heat within the organization; *mindful leadership is not an approach, strategy, or*

Text Box 8.3

> Then there is the continual degree of disagreement, the philosophical divide that is larger than what anyone thought possible, and the countless times when meetings turn into long tirades of philosophical comments and other wanderings of the mind. Such are the descriptions that are part of the discussions in class. These are the issues that divide the staff. Students in class ask the questions about the possibilities that can change the culture of the school to be more collegial, inclusive, harmonious, socially just, and productive.
>
> Just below the surface of the conversations runs another thread, and that is the one in which many aspiring leaders in the classes question whether or not it is worth becoming a leader. Concerns are listed for the attrition rates of principals and worry about who might take their place, particularly to find leaders with experience. Aspiring leaders are not the only ones questioning—the practicing leaders often question about the stress of unending agendas, responding to the daily barrage of questions, requests, conflicts, and challenges. The conversations sometimes stall out, with what appears to be some resignation that things will not change.

technique. Mindful leadership involves qualities of compassion, listening, being with, awareness, acceptance, trust, and patience—all strongly associated with emotional intelligence factors such as empathy and self-awareness. Because of these concepts, mindfulness practice contributes to peace, harmony, understanding, and inclusion. People's personal feelings matter, and their personal narratives are heard with an emphasis on nonjudgment and nonreactivity.

How Mindfulness Helps with Staying Calm in the Moment

Finding the calm in the middle of the storm is perhaps one of the big gifts of mindfulness meditation because it allows for leaders to pause throughout the day as the day unfolds and problems emerge. Gaining perspective throughout the day, stopping the intense reaction, and allowing stillness is a way to step away from the endless cycle of stress, and allowing the calm to surface.

What could a leader do to encourage using the pause button during stressful situations? Practice, practice and more practice of mindfulness allows for a more automatic response, with a leader thinking of compassion instead of anger, empathy instead of judgment, listening instead of arguing or insisting, attention instead of distracted observation, or stillness instead of immediately reacting. The repeated practice of meditation instills a sense of pausing for the present moment and accepting what is, as opposed to fighting it.

To step back, be with, listen to, and avoid the judging, gives a view that is altogether different, one in which other viewpoints can be understood. When people examine the typical automatic reaction versus the more mindful response, it is like a light turning on in the room. Why? Everyone has experienced the cascade that can escalate after receiving another person's critical reaction. A mindful response offers understanding in how to be more accepting and less combative.

Mindfulness practice allows for a response to threat without combat and the propensity to escalate the negative or downward spiral. This does not mean that the mindful response is without pain. There aren't too many people who would be glad to hear that subordinates have viewed their actions negatively. Effective leaders will still feel the pain of betrayal, anguish over being attacked for new concepts or initiatives, and feeling marginalized on the job (Heifetz & Linsky, 2002). The pain of rejection is an understandable first response, one that can be modified when the person receiving the information can sit with the information, giving it time and space.

It is important to recognize that mindfulness practice does not take away the pain of difficult situations; in fact, it can allow the pain to be more fully experienced in the initial stages. Denying or resisting a problem never solves it, and often worsens it. By accepting what is, and allowing the reality to be observed, the path to an effective resolution, and one that serves the leader and the organization is possible.

Educational Leaders Who Practice Finding the Calm in the Middle of the Storm

- Model the possibility for others to emulate
- Give themselves the gift of peace in the moment
- Demonstrate peaceful resolutions to problems in the schools and school district
- Have an increased possibility of a willingness to stay in the profession of school leadership—*finding calm in stress is correlated with resilience*
- Practice self-care—it is essential to learn how to find calm in stressful situations
- Inspire others to seek calm, peace, and stillness in challenging times
- Learn to trust in their ability to not just ride out the stress, but effectively attend to it
- Develop patience that it takes to stay focused on the calm when the stakes are high and the problems are surging

GETTING BACK ON THE BIKE

Leaders deal with conflict, crisis, and change, often at a relentless pace. It isn't possible to be a leader without facing these crises. The metaphor of learning to ride a bike is parallel with the issues that leaders face.

Leaders start off excited to be chosen for the position. They are sure of many things and unsure of others. Their training from the institution is like the training wheels—they come off quickly when one is in the leader's chair; they are now alone in that chair, office, and position. They are learning to ride on their own. The new ride is exciting, freeing, maybe even terrifying.

The ride is not without bumps. The driver on the bike is often involved with wildly over steering, until the rider is thrown from the bike. The first fall hurts. What happened? Things were going along OK, and now the rider is on the ground, with a skinned knee and maybe even some embarrassment to show for it. There are people watching on the sidelines, and it appears that one of them might even be laughing.

But the intention to ride propels the rider beyond the pain or fear of falling. Almost immediately, the rider gets back on the bike. The ride goes better this time, *until the next fall.* But now the rider knows from experience that falls can lead to a new beginning; the pain is not permanent, and the lessons learned fuel a better ride the next time. That is until the next fall. Eventually there are fewer falls, infrequent, and yet always possible with a stone or pothole in the road, or a deep rut along the side.

The trick for riders as for leaders is to get back on the bike. Resilience is learned from our problems and our falls, just as it is possible to learn emotional intelligence. How is this learning fostered? By having the intention to listen, learn, be patient, attend to, not judge self or others, be compassionate, trust, accept reality, and let go—the qualities of mindfulness practice.

We learn that the shift in attitude often follows the shift in behavior, in this case a behavior of sitting in stillness, whether bored or restless, and just following the breath or the thoughts, with the focus on the present moment. *There is sense making through practice. The practice teaches people to turn in to the problem instead of running from it, seeing what we observe, becoming aware of, and noticing the present moment.*

Mindfulness helps teach people to pause and take a breath, which helps those who practice to be able to control their thoughts. For example, if a leader were suddenly in a situation with an irate parent, one where the leader feels criticized or attacked, the mindfulness practice of nonjudgment, compassion, and listening can help the leader step back and listen to what the parent is saying, with a spirit of wanting to know what is behind the complaint, as opposed to a vigorous defense or dismissal.

Mindfulness practice also helps people to change the perpetual chatter of the mind, with the storylines that often accompany the intense feelings or emotions. Because of the practice of sitting and being with the thoughts and emotions, people learn to develop patience and understanding, qualities that help to control mind chatter, often referred to as "monkey mind" where thoughts tend to dominate in a fast-paced, endless bombardment.

In doing so, people often uncover feelings that have been buried, ones that may be hurtful. Ultimately it is possible to learn that profound healing is possible through this practice, although it may feel a lot worse before it feels better. *Slower is faster in this regard; complexity is reduced to simplicity—the simplicity of stillness and quiet. Distraction gives way to awareness, clutter to spaciousness.*

Leaders need to be aware of the potholes in the road, and know that they will feel the entire range of experience from joy to sadness with the job, and that even if these emotions *throw the leader from the bike*, the leader will be able to get up and ride again. Leaders need to be encouraged and provided with training and support to learn how to push the pause button, learning the process of mindfulness.

Richie Davidson (2011) presented convincing data of the power of mindfulness to transform and build resilience, happiness, and compassion; he stated:

> We are not indelibly fixed in our current state, but rather these are characteristics that can be transformed. There is a very precious and important convergence of that idea with the modern concept of neuroplasticity—the notion that the brain can change in response to experience and training—a convergence that provides a foundation for us as scientists to go forward in a truly novel and integrative way. (pp. 23–24)

Mindfulness practice is correlated with the strengthening of the positive qualities of empathy and compassion, including the changes in brain structure and function (Davidson et al., 2012). Empathy involves the ability to "feel what others are feeling" (Davidson & Begley, 2012, p. 55). Compassion refers to the ability to send "love and kindness" to someone who is suffering (Germer, 2009, p. 33). In this sense, compassion is often viewed as a verb, implying action. Mindfulness-based stress reduction is correlated with an enhanced resilience after stressful encounters (Davidson & Begley, 2012). Mindfulness plays an important part in recovering from stressful situations because of its relation to producing emotional balance in people (Davidson & Begley).

Educational Leaders Who Practice Getting "Back on the Bike"

- Demonstrate that failures or problems are not final
- Model self-compassion in their willingness to move beyond whatever threw them from the bike in the first place
- Develop trust in their own abilities to lead
- Develop patience in being fully present and attending to what occurred in the school or school district
- And perhaps so essential to the theme of hope illustrated with the concept of Mindfulness for Educational Leaders . . .
- Model what is often described as an "American way" of never giving up— of a comeback story, a second chance, an encore, a redemption

THE POWER OF "AND"

Mindfulness practice makes powerful use of the word *"and"* as opposed to *"but."* The word "and" connects the positive and the negative experiences and includes the problems, challenges, and difficulties instead of being rejected, overlooked, or denied. The word "and" has a different connotation and power from the word, "but." When people hear, *"That was a great job on the project but . . ."* they know that it wasn't a great job. The "but" always cancels out anything affirmative. The "and" however, builds bridges and offers new vistas.

Leaders deal with the ambiguity of challenge, and yet with mindfulness practice there can be a melding or integration of feelings that are *not the either-or, east-west, right-wrong, or in-out opposites.* Mindfulness allows for different perspectives that accept and acknowledge all that is in the landscape, recognizing that it is possible to have a dichotomy of experience.

Educational Leaders Who Mindfully Practice the "Power of AND" Know That They Can Be:

> *Worried and still at peace;*
> *Broken and still OK;*
> *Alone and also together;*
> *Sad and yet content;*
> *Scattered and still in the moment;*
> *Knocked down and still standing;*
> *Lost and also found.*

How is this possible? Certainly not overnight, or without challenge or pain; mindfulness helps with the restoration that impacts resilience.

MINDFUL LEADERSHIP AND THE HOME COURT ADVANTAGE

Leaders' struggles are in the public eye, with friends and resisters watching. Boyatzis and McKee (2005) began their book with a chapter entitled "Great leaders move us" (p. 1). People may understand that concept, although the means to make that happen may be elusive. People also understand that people are often watching and waiting to be "moved" or inspired while we are in the middle of a conflict, again all in the public eye. There is more pressure and perhaps a feeling that one is alone "on the mat" or on "the stage," again, with all eyes focused on the leader.

As leaders practice mindfulness, there can be a reframing of the experiences, thoughts, and feelings that are associated with leadership. Leaders who become attuned to practicing acceptance, awareness, compassion and self-compassion, patience, trust, nonreactivity, nonjudgment, being fully present, and listening may present differently to others. This way of being extends compassion to others in an inviting way.

Educational leaders can help others going through a professional crisis by just being with them, listening, not judging, offering supportive space for them to find their own way back home, a *home court advantage*. Mindfulness helps with the cultivation of compassion, which is the action of empathy. People can offer that home court advantage to other leaders with a compassionate outreach to others in crisis, without looking away or trying to solve the problem for them.

This book began by describing the incredible challenges that leaders face; the close offers means for responding to those challenges. It seems that as people learn to take better care of themselves, they may also see the connection to taking care of others, all possible with mindfulness.

Text Box 8.4

The concept that exemplifies this concept is one I frequently shared with students in the school when I was high school principal—the concept is that of *home court advantage*. We all understand what happens with home court advantage when the players feel supported and even revered, often regardless of the score. Fans in the stands cheer and yell for the home team, resulting in what is commonly understood as the home court advantage. With home court advantage there is a feeling of respect and admiration, one that is important for educational leaders, and the good news is that we are the ones who can give that to each other. It's a feeling that is conveyed, "I've got your back with this one." That's the Home Court Advantage.

Text Box 8.5

Leaders have my highest regard. I watch and listen to the stories of aspiring and practicing leaders in my graduate classes and am reminded of a moment of high regard I had for the wrestlers—the ones who step out in public, on the mat, and risk being pinned each time while an audience watches. This moment struck me one time while I was in the bleachers watching a wrestling match. Sure, the whole team sat on the sidelines but they were not on the mat. Yes, they were cheering, as were the people in the stands, but being alone on the mat is a very different type of experience. Two wrestlers were on the mat, with one official. Everyone else was a spectator. I see the parallels with leaders who are often *alone on the mat* in the public eye despite the teams they represent and their other personal or professional connections. Educational leaders are not in actual wrestling matches, although, on occasions, it may feel that way, as people use force to prevail in what could be a win-lose contest. A home court advantage offers a sense of enthusiastic support for the leader in what may feel like a public contest or showdown.

We can help educational leaders support each other through networking, a type of collective support and understanding for the stress that others are experiencing. Networking can foster a web of compassionate understanding. The resource section of this book contains a sample note that can be sent to other school leaders—it is a "quick" way to let leaders know they are being given the home court advantage. We know that many leaders feel isolated and stressed; a note or communication of empathy can make an incredible difference.

MINDFUL LEADERSHIP—THE POSSIBILITIES

Mindful leadership, as defined in this book, is the integration of constructs of mindfulness practice, with emotional, social, and resonant leadership, informed by the research from neuroscience. Mindful leadership embraces the interconnectedness and interdependencies of mindful practice. Thus, the *practice* of mindful practice benefits the person in the moment, and it has an impact that is possible in the *practice* of leadership. With practice, the cultivation of the qualities inherent in the constructs such as acceptance, awareness and being fully present; listening, trust, patience, nonreactivity, nonjudgment, compassion and self-compassion can be developed; it is a cycle of growth, all possible from being in the moment on purpose, practicing awareness and attention without judgment or criticism.

The conception of mindful leadership can be understood by comparing a paradigm of how leadership is often conveyed with the possibilities of mindful leadership (see table 8.1).

Mindful leadership is like an awakening of the senses, one that can fuel a leader during days of challenge. It's not just the relaxation or absence of stress; relaxation can only do so much. It's the understanding of how the practice of mindfulness can also inform the practice of leadership. The practice of mindfulness has multiple qualities—it comes to life through experience. There are many gifts with mindfulness practice—stress reduction, qualities that relate to effective leadership, resilience, and importantly, the attributes associated with legacy leadership, the ones for which many leaders would want to be remembered. If these efforts are only engaged for resume building, and not personal growth and serving others, they do not make the final criteria of legacy work. Emotional and social intelligence traits serve others.

As seen in table 8.2, mindfulness practice has benefits that are associated with one's personal and professional life. The same qualities that build effective personal relationships add to the benefit in the organization. It is easy to see, from the chart above, how compassion, for example, is a benefit in a

Table 8.1   New Descriptions of Leadership.

Previous Descriptions of Leadership	Mindful Leadership
Striving	Letting go
Doing	Being
Talking	Listening
Making things happen	Accepting reality
Clutter	Spaciousness
Judging	Compassionate understanding
Telling	Hearing
Multitasking	Single tasking
Distracted thinking about "to-do" list	Being in the moment
Directing	Accepting
Busyness	Stillness
Distracted preoccupation	Attentive awareness

Source: Wells (2015, p. 14).

Table 8.2   Qualities of Mindful Leadership.

Qualities	Informed By
Personal	**Conceptual**
Listening, empathy, compassion, hearing, patience, awareness, nonjudgment, acceptance, being fully present	Research based, theory, models, literature
Professional	**Experiential**
Listening, empathy, compassion, hearing, patience, beginner's mind, trust, awareness, acceptance, being fully present, compassion	Practice; being with; meditating, time in stillness

Source: Wells, (2015).

personal or professional relationship. Yet, in leadership training, the emphases might be on knowledge, concepts, information, technical as opposed to emotional or social skills, and the dispositions of leaders. In the literature of leadership there are different descriptions of what is important. Organizations that are building the capacity in the workplace have a distinct focus on social and emotional intelligence, and resonant leadership.

What are some of the lessons learned from mindfulness for leaders?

- **It might get worse before it gets better—stay with it**
- **The way in to the situation leads to the way out**
- **Faster is slower; slower is faster**
- **Being is the new doing**
- **Quiet is the new language;** *listening* **is the new talking**
- **Busyness is not equated with productivity**
- **Getting "back on the bike" through mindfulness practice builds resilience**
- **The pain of failing can be a great teacher**

I began this book with a quote from a physician: I close with another from Helen, Reiss, Harvard Medical School (2010),

> Empathy is an important component of clinical competence. Empathic physicians can obtain critical information and insights that affect quality of care and, ultimately, medical outcomes. Evidence supports physiological benefits of empathic relationships, including better immune function, shorter postsurgery hospital stays, fewer asthma attacks, stronger placebo response, and shorter duration of colds. (p. 1605)

If the empathic relationship of a physician can result in the benefits listed above, what would the benefits include of school leaders who are empathic, patient, compassionate, fully present in the moment, nonjudgmental,

Text Box 8.6

The feedback that I have from graduate students is that mindfulness practice is making a difference in their lives. I hope to hear that mindful leadership will have a similar impact, offering a view of the world in the present moment, one that was somehow obscured because of the stress and activity of the busy leader. Mindful leadership can present a different way—a *leader of being* that offers hope and inspires by example. The view of the present moment can offer new vistas, ones that include a different way of being for mindful leaders and the people and organizations they serve.

accepting, and aware? I look for future research to report on the benefits of mindful leadership to impact and influence the culture of the school to actualize its goals and vision.

I believe we are on the threshold of this new form of leadership, made possible through mindfulness. Perhaps in offering this information to educational leaders, they will feel hope to stay the course, keep their commitment for their own personal health, help others in the field, improve their practice, and feel that they can thrive in a vocation that is their calling.

After all, educational leaders know that there will be storms. ***Storms are OK. They give you a chance to use your anchor*** (Wells, 2015, p. 18).

Mindfulness provides the hope of an anchor, one, that with practice, can lift an educational leader to learn how to practice self-care, develop resilience, build the qualities that we hope for in our eulogy, serve others, and stay the course of leading. Yes, it is a lot, and, all of it is possible. *May you remember you have the anchor . . .*

KEY CONCEPTS

- Busy educational leaders need to make time for mindfulness practice, there will otherwise never be time for practice
- Mindfulness is a practice, a discipline that develops over time
- We only have now for living and experiencing life—mindfulness helps us to remember that
- A mindful moment can break a cycle of "24/7" connectivity for an educational leader with peace and stillness in the smallest sliver of time
- Mindfulness for educational leaders is about learning how to be with what is occurring, without judgment or criticism
- Finding calm in the middle of a storm is possible when one enters into stillness, allowing the calm of the moment to enter awareness
- Even in times of challenge, mindfulness teaches us to lean into the storm, allowing for insights. Even the "eye of the storm" offers a respite from the turbulence—all possible through mindfulness practice
- Mindfulness helps educational leaders gain perspective, leading with compassion, attention, and listening while the winds of the storms blow
- Resilience is built from the fall "off the bike" when leaders learn how to steer through rough pavement and ruts along the side of the road
- *Failures are not final—self-compassion and mindfulness practice make this very clear*
- Empathy offers a powerful "home court advantage" to everyone in the school or school district
- Mindfulness constructs come to life through experience and practice

- The pain of failing can be a great teacher
- Mindful awareness lets leaders know that they can be knocked down and still stand tall

Final Thoughts

Now that you have an introduction to mindfulness practice and the different ways you can include practice, it is important to know that there are many ways to continue and deepen your practice. You can:

- Copy and work with the various practices included at the end of this book—they are intended to be used multiple times, depending on what you want to reinforce
- Consider buying some of the resources listed in this book to learn more about mindfulness, and use the CDs for meditation practice
- The best way to experience the impact of mindfulness is just that—experience it through practice, practice, and more practice, whether it be moments or minutes in the day
- Consider taking a Mindfulness Based Stress Reduction (MBSR) 8-week program, available online or with neighborhood programs
- Attend day-long retreats to practice with others and enter into stillness
- Consider other retreats such as those focusing on self-compassion

There are two significant symbols in this book that encourage and lift me—they are the *bike* from the message about getting back on the bike, and the *anchor*, the one that refers to the breath and mindfulness practice—both the *bike* and the *anchor* provide a vision of forward motion and resilience.

The acronym for anchor is one that might remind you of the essential learning in this book:

A—Accept what is in the present moment—be fully present for it
N—Nonjudgment of self and others
C—Compassion and self-compassion
H—Have intention, and *hear* what is there to be heard—practice listening
O—Observe, notice, sense, and feel what is happening
R—Renew and restore—this happens with practice.

You are the only one who can give yourself the gift of practice, of learning to take care of yourself. *No one else can do this for you.*

If you have fallen, *get back on the bike—you were made to ride.*

Appendix

Guide to the Mindfulness Practices

The appendix includes the following practices—some relating to the work environment and others relate to practices for stress reduction or the mindfulness constructs.

These are some of the examples that I use as part of class explanations, trainings, or presentations with professional organizations.

Survey—for ending the book
Checklist for taking care of yourself
Tune-up—saying "No" to and "Yes" to
Constructs—importance of; practicing at work
Mindful Leadership description
Listening to wake-up calls
Survey about stress and mindfulness; Key to survey
Practice for being in the moment
Practice for letting go
Practice for cultivating compassion
Practice for reducing tension
Practice for dealing with conflict
Leadership—cultivating self-compassion
Practice—cultivating mindful moments
Practice for feeling anxious, sad, or experiencing tension or worry
Practice for cultivating listening
Sample mindfulness meditation practices
Samples for beginning a meeting

Survey—Ending the Book

Please complete the same survey that you took at the beginning of the book. See how your answers have changed.

Directions: Answer each statement to the extent with which you agree or disagree with each.

Key   1. Strongly Disagree   2. Disagree   3. Agree   4. Strongly Agree

		1	2	3	4
1.	I am sure of what to do to manage the stress from work	1	2	3	4
2.	I know how to practice self-compassion	1	2	3	4
3.	I take some time out for mindful moments throughout the day at work	1	2	3	4
4.	I feel patient with things that unfold during the day at work	1	2	3	4
5.	I practice self-care efforts like mindfulness	1	2	3	4
6.	I tend to criticize myself when I make a mistake	1	2	3	4
7.	I tend to deny, project, or blame when I feel attacked by criticism	1	2	3	4
8.	I recognize messages, or "wake-up calls" as they happen at work	1	2	3	4
9.	I feel compassion for people in my school or school district	1	2	3	4
10.	I find it difficult to concentrate and be fully in the present moment at work	1	2	3	4
11.	I sometimes find it hard to empathize with situations I encounter at school or the school district	1	2	3	4
12.	I notice that I don't always listen to what is happening at school or in the school district because I am overwhelmed, distracted, or preoccupied	1	2	3	4
13.	I find moments of stillness during the workday	1	2	3	4
14.	I worry about my ever-growing "to-do" list	1	2	3	4
15.	I spend some time worrying about or regretting things I have done or left undone at work	1	2	3	4

Figure A.1   Survey—Ending the Book.

Options to Consider—Checklist for Taking Care of Yourself

A planning guide to include mindfulness practice. Record what you have completed at the end of the week.

I . . .
began each day with a 5-minute meditation last week _____
included some time for mindful moments at work _____
used my breathing to calm down in a stressful moment _____
set limits and boundaries for when I will respond to e-mail messages

_____

closed out my day with some peaceful mindfulness practice

_____

listened to some mindfulness CDs to enter into practice _____
practiced some Hatha yoga from a DVD or a live session _____
ate mindfully at lunch, taking the time to just eat, nothing more

_____

noticed when I need to take some time to slow my world down and enter
    into stillness _____
practiced self-compassion when I had some problems at work

_____

noticed if I am judging myself, and if I am, do not judge the judging

_____

focused on the present moment, and stopped thoughts of worry about
    tomorrow or regrets from yesterday _____

This survey asks you to think about how you take care of yourself with mindfulness. The take away: Put your own oxygen mask on first; mindfulness helps with that.

Periodic Tune-up—Thoughts for you to think about that may be interfering with your mindfulness practice.

Periodic Tune-up—Saying NO

What are you willing to say "NO" to? What—list example	List how to accomplish this
Unplug with texts . . .	
Unplug from e-mail . . .	
Unplug from the computer . . . or social media	
Unplug from the smartphone . . .	
Think twice about doing . . .	
Say "No" to . . .	

Periodic Tune-up—Saying YES

What are you willing to say "Yes" to?	When and how
Experiencing a mindful moment . . .	
Pushing the "pause button" when I know I need to . . .	

Entering into stillness/mindfulness at work	
Entering into stillness/mindfulness at home	
Practicing what I need for self-care . . .	
Practicing any of the mindfulness constructs	

Sample Practice—Working with the Constructs

Construct	Why this construct is important at work.
Acceptance	
Awareness/Being fully present	
Compassion/Self-Compassion	
Letting go	
Listening	
Nonjudgment	
Nonreactivity	

Patience	
Trust	

Sample Practice—Working with the Constructs

Construct	Describe one thing you could do to practice this construct at work.
Acceptance	
Awareness/Being fully present	
Compassion/Self-Compassion	
Letting go	
Listening	
Nonjudgment	
Nonreactivity	
Patience	
Trust	

MINDFUL LEADERSHIP IS:

Instead of	Mindful Leadership Approaches	Instead of acting
Unaware; not seeing the reality of the situation	←Acceptance→	Blaming others
Preoccupied or distracted	←Awareness→	Refusing to accept reality
Regretting the past	←Being Fully Present→	Worrying about tomorrow
Not caring or listening to someone in need	←Compassion→	Judging + criticism
Not caring enough to be interested	←Letting Go→	Holding on
Disregarding	←Listening→	Interrupting or telling your story
Not observing or being aware of a situation not on the 'radar screen'	←Patience→	Lashing out
Denying; avoiding	←Responding→	Angry outburst; reacting
Disbelief; disregard	←Trust→	Duplicity; Not doing what you say

Figure A.2

PRACTICE

Noticing Default Mechanisms—A Key to Listening to the Wake-Up Calls for Leaders

Noticing default mechanisms that are often automatic is important for a leader. Mindfulness can interrupt the cycle with another option.

Default Habit	Describe one thing you could do to reframe, from mindfulness practice. What is one viable option to the default habit?
Denying, blaming	
Being preoccupied, distracted	
Judging or criticizing someone	
Judging or criticizing self	
Not trusting in your own ability	
Holding on to past resentments	
Worrying about tomorrow or the to-do list	
Reacting to what is happening	

Survey about Work and Mindfulness

Directions: Read each prompt and respond according to your initial reaction as to how you feel during or about your workplace. The key is on the next page.

Key   1. Hardly ever   2. Sometimes   3. Fair amount   4. A great deal
         5. Almost always

Begin with this question: To what degree do you-Feel stress at work? Next, answer the following prompts about work- To what extent do you:	1	2	3	4	5
1.	Feel preoccupied during the day at work	1	2	3	4	5
2.	Accept situations for what they are as they happen at work	1	2	3	4	5
3.	Feel angry at things that happen during the day at work	1	2	3	4	5
4.	Feel patient with things that unfold during the day at work	1	2	3	4	5
5.	Feel judgmental with the people you interact with during the day	1	2	3	4	5
6.	Wish you could leave, retire, or get another work position	1	2	3	4	5
7.	Long for the weekend during the weekday	1	2	3	4	5
8.	Begin dreading Monday on Sunday	1	2	3	4	5
9.	Feel compassion for people in your department	1	2	3	4	5
10.	Feel you are able to listen to others, really hearing what they have to say at work	1	2	3	4	5
11.	Think about work when you are at home	1	2	3	4	5
12.	Regret things that have happened in the past at work	1	2	3	4	5
13.	Think about all you have to do at work when you are at home	1	2	3	4	5
14.	Worry about how you can accomplish everything you need to get done at work	1	2	3	4	5
15.	Deny or avoid some of the problems you are facing at work	1	2	3	4	5

Figure A.3

Survey About Work and Mindfulness Key

Directions: First, review the degree to which you feel stress at work, and note the level at which you feel that stress. Then, review each of the fifteen options, noting the level of stress that you feel for each. Compare the levels of stress according to the constructs listed below noting which of the areas you equate the most stress.

You can see what constructs are areas that relate most directly to your stress levels, signaling areas for practice and compassion.

For each question, the construct is:

1. awareness, being in the moment
2. acceptance
3. patience
4. nonjudgment, compassion
5. nonjudgment, compassion
6. being in the moment, acceptance
7. being in the moment
8. being in the moment
9. compassion, nonjudgment
10. listening
11. being in the moment
12. acceptance, self-compassion
13. being in the moment, acceptance
14. being in the moment
15. acceptance, patience

The bottom line is in determining what level of stress you are experiencing at work. Would you classify your stress as:

Slight _____

Moderate _____

Worrisome _____

Overwhelming _____

PRACTICE

For Being in the Moment

Changing the focus from seeing the entire landscape, to viewing the present moment

Describe the reality of your landscape:

What in this landscape causes you concern?

Mindful practice asks that you:
Have the intention to give your attention to the present moment;
Without judgment or criticism;
Watching feelings and thoughts and just being aware of them; and
Watching the feelings and thoughts come and go, listening to them with compassion and awareness, trusting in your own ability to be with all that is happening.
Sitting in stillness, watch the landscape change as thoughts and feelings enter the mind.

As you practice the above and place your attention to the present moment, are you able to reduce the size of your "landscape" and look instead at what you are experiencing in the moment as you sit in stillness?
Or,
Are you able to allow yourself to just be with the situation of concern? Watch as the feelings and thoughts come and go, like clouds in the sky. Just be aware and give those feelings some room, without trying to control them. Watch for the insights from this practice.

PRACTICE

For Letting Go

Instead of:
Holding on to ruminating about, replaying a conversation or meeting that didn't work well, or anything else from the past that enters your mind without invitation.

Describe the thought you would like to place in the "letting go" file:

Mindfulness suggests the attention to the issue as the beginning place for letting go. Give this issue your attention.

The change is in your response to the issue, as opposed to an automatic reaction. Do this without criticism. Put your attention on the issue.

The problem invading your mind is like a rain cloud, one that comes into view and leaves again. Watch as the rain cloud leaves your thought space, exclaiming to yourself that you are releasing it. Let the thought go. Sit for a moment, feeling the peace of the release.

If the issue you are trying to release wanders back into your mind, know that this is what the mind does. Without criticism or blame, repeat the steps listed above until you are able to let go of the issue.

SAMPLE PRACTICE

For Cultivating Compassion

Think of the situation or person in which you are feeling judgment or anger.

Sit with those feelings, being alert to when the feelings of judgment enter. When judgment comes, be aware of it without judging the judgment.

Consider the voice or personal narrative of the other person—you already know your own.

Reframe the storyline you have developed about the other person and replace it with statements like "Compassion" or "Understanding."

What might the other person's personal narrative include? How about the background of this person, including possible personal history. What from this person's background might be influencing that point of view?

Add to the understanding of the person by acknowledging how this person most likely wants what all people want: to be happy, whole, and recognized. List the possible common wants of that person, and finish with the statement, "Just like me." So if you have deduced that the person just wants to be understood and accepted, finish with, "Just like me."

Consider your current feelings for the person or situation listed on this sheet. Have your feeling changed in any way?

PRACTICE

For Reducing Tension

Sit for a few moments in a position that represents your dignity—one that allows for your attention to the moment.

Allow your eyes to close gently and take a few deep breaths, just noticing the inhale and exhale.

Pay attention to anywhere in your body where some tension or pressure exists, this may be in the neck, the shoulders, and lower back, places that seem to hold the tensions that we often feel.

Be aware of the pressures or tension you are feeling, without criticism or judgment.

With your next inhalation, breathe a deep breath and send it to the area of your pain, just giving it some spaciousness. Allow that breath to sur-round the pain.

With your next exhalation, invite the pain or tension to leave your body.

Continue this process for a few series of inhalations and exhalations, then allow yourself to sit in stillness.

Accept and face any pain that may remain, not resisting or fighting it. You may want to focus instead on your breath, watching the cool air that enters your nostrils and the warm air of the exhalation.

Or, you can allow yourself to be with any of the tension that remains, just observing it without trying to control it.

Let your body sit in stillness, relaxing the muscles throughout the body.

Repeat as needed. Tension has a way of returning for our attention.

PRACTICE

For Dealing with Conflict

Describe the situation of the conflict:

Be aware of the present moment, just sit with the conflict, without trying to solve, deny, repair, or avoid it.

What are you aware of? Be aware of all your feelings. Does this conflict reside in any part of your body, such as the heart, head, or gut?

Listening to the other point of view in the conflict, without judgment or criticism, what do you hear?

Listening to yourself without judgment of criticism, what do you hear?

Sitting in stillness, what do you observe?

Where are you now with the conflict?

What are your insights or observations?

PRACTICE

Cultivating Leadership in Self-Compassion

Call into your mind a situation in which you would like to rewind the tape of something you were involved with at work . . .

Let yourself feel what you are feeling . . . just be aware, and allow what you are feeling.

Talk to yourself as you would to a good friend—what would you say to your best friend about the same situation?

Self-compassion teaches us that there is common humanity in the problems we face. What, from your story reinforces this concept? What have you learned from this experience that brings you to a new place of growth, insights, or wisdom?

SAMPLE PRACTICE

Cultivating Mindful Moments

Mindful Moments are one way to cultivate peace amidst the rush of the day. Think of some of the things you do daily, often on autopilot, and replace those activities with mindful moments such as the ones listed below.

Some typical autopilot activities:
Morning shower
Walking the dog
Making coffee or tea
Driving in traffic
Washing your hands
Eating breakfast

Replace each autopilot activity with a mindful moment.

For example, if your morning shower is the time where you review the agenda for the day, replace the frenzy with a focus on the miracle of the shower, the hot water and the feel of the water on your back, washing your hair with intention and awareness, etc. *Be in the moment with the activity.*

List some ways that you could include mindful moments in your daily world. You may want to develop some of these, or develop your own list.

Walking from the parking lot to your office

Washing or rinsing dishes

Dressing

Drinking your morning beverage

Walking in the stairwell

Eating a piece of chocolate

SAMPLE PRACTICE

For Feeling Anxious, Sad, Tense, or Worried

Describe what you are feeling

Be aware of your feelings—sit with them without judging or criticizing them, yourself, or others.

What are you aware of?

Listen to your observations.

Without judging or criticizing yourself, give voice to your feelings—the entire range. Include thoughts of sadness or anxiety without repressing or denying them.

Notice if the feelings of anxiety or sadness seem to reside in any part of your body, your heart, heard, or gut, for example.

Breathe into the area that is challenging for you and send your breath deeply into that worry, inviting it to leave.

Let yourself engage in a slight smile, or a half-smile. Note how this feels for you. A half-smile can push away some of the feelings like fight, fight, or freeze.

Sit in stillness, just being with what you are feeling.
Where are you now? What are you observing? What are the insights from the awareness?

PRACTICE

Cultivating Leadership in Listening

First, just settle in, being aware of what there is to be heard. Listen to the sounds without trying to search for them.

When your mind begins to wander, just bring your attention back to the sounds in your room without judgment or criticism.

Just being aware of the sounds without judging or evaluating them, note what you are hearing, being aware, and accepting.

In your work setting, practice by listening to another person, listening to hear, not to respond, fix, or solve the issue at hand.

Just observe what you are hearing without judging, analyzing, or criticizing. Is this difficult for you?

Just *listen to hear* when the mind wanders to thinking of your response.

What have you observed from these practices? What are you aware of?

Sample Mindfulness Meditation Practice

Find a comfortable place to sit. Close off your computer screen, with cell phone on airport mode so you do not hear it if it pulses.

When ready, let your eyes gently close. Feel yourself in the chair, your feet on the floor; just be aware of sitting in the moment, in that space, at that time. Let your body relax and feel the stillness.

Notice your breath as it enters and leaves the body. Just pay attention and observe without judging or criticizing yourself or others. Notice the breath and when your mind wanders, just bring it back to the breath, again without judging or criticism.

Let your body relax—raise your shoulders up to your ears and let them drop, feeling a deeper level of peace and stillness.

If you note any tension in your back, shoulders, or neck, just send your breath to that area and give some space around it, allowing that tension to leave as you exhale.

Return you attention to your breath, noticing it as it enters and leaves your body. This is time that you are giving just for yourself. Let your body feel at peace.

When you are ready, open your eyes and continue to sit in stillness, savoring the stillness of the present moment until you are ready to return to the outside world.

Sample Mindfulness Practices for Beginning Meetings

I'm wondering if we could just sit for a few moments in stillness before beginning this meeting, allowing ourselves the gift of quiet of the present moment to surface, leaving behind the rush of getting here and all that that involves. So, please put your cell phones on airport mode—this is time just for you.

In a few minutes, you could add:

Thank you.

Or, on occasion you might add:

Thank you. Our commitment is to find ways for us to support efforts to find the stillness in the moment that will allow us to be fully present.

Another example, when people have participated in the practice, and are aware of the intentions:

Let's just take some time to settle in before the meeting, just being present in the moment. (Allow a minute or two for stillness.)

Followed by: Thank you.

Mindfulness Resources

JON KABAT-ZINN SERIES—CDS

Series 1: Body Scan; Mindful Yoga; Sitting Meditation; Mindful Yoga 2
Series 2: Sitting Meditations; Lying Down Meditations; Mountain Meditation/ Lake Meditation; Silence with Bells
Series 3: Breathscape and Bodyscape Meditations; Soundscape, Mindscape, and Dying Before You Die Meditations; Nowscape (Choiceless Awareness) and Walking Meditations; Heartscape (Lovingkindness) and Lifescape (Everyday Life) Meditations

MEDITATIONS FOR EMOTIONAL HEALING—TARA BRACH

Mindfulness Meditation: Nine Guided Practices to Awaken Presence and Open Your Heart—Tara Brach

Books by Jon Kabat-Zinn

Kabat-Zinn. (1994). *Wherever you go there you are: Mindfulness meditation in everyday life.* New York, NY: Hyperion.
Kabat-Zinn, J. (2005). *Coming to our senses: Healing ourselves and the world through medicine.* New York, NY: Hyperion.
Kabat-Zinn, J. (2009). *Full catastrophe living: Using the wisdom of your body and mind to face stress, pain, and illness (15th anniversary edition).* New York, NY: Random House.

Mindfulness Books with CDs

Kabat-Zinn, J. (2012). *Mindfulness for beginners: Reclaiming the present moment—and your life.* Boulder, CO: Sounds True, Inc.

Includes CD with Shortened Meditations

Williams, M., Teasdale, J., Segal, Z., & Kabat-Zinn, J. (2007). *The mindful way through depression: Freeing yourself from chronic unhappiness.* New York, NY: The Guilford Press. Includes CD with shortened meditations—includes a 30-minute body scan.

Mindfulness Books

Baer, R. (2014). *The practicing happiness workbook.* Oakland, CA: New Harbinger Publications. Full of helpful strategies to cultivate wellness and joy.

Brantley, J. (2007). *Calming your anxious mind.* Oakland, CA: New Harbinger Publications, Inc. Great strategies for relaxation.

Boyce, B. (Ed.) (2011). *The mindfulness revolution: Leading psychologists, scientists, artists, and meditation teachers on the power of mindfulness in daily life.* Boston, MA: Shambhala Sun. Outstanding chapters written by the leading authors of mindfulness.

Brown, V. & Olson, K. (2015). *The mindful school leader: Practices to transform your leadership and school.* Thousand Oaks, CA: Corwin Press. Wonderful book that highlights vignettes of educational leaders in the field who use mindfulness to make a difference in their lives and those of students.

Carroll, M. (2007). *The mindful leader: Ten principles for bringing out the best in ourselves and others.* Boston, MA: Trumpeter. Shares excellent strategies for working with mindful presence.

Chaskalson, M. (2011). *The mindful workplace: Developing resilient individuals and resonant organizations with MBSR.* Chichester, West Sussex, UK: John Wiley & Sons, Ltd.

Davidson, R. J. & Begley, S. (2012). *The emotional life of your brain.* New York, NY: Hudson Street Press.

Eblin, S. (2014). *Overworked and overwhelmed: The mindfulness alternative.* Hoboken, NJ: John Wiley Publishing.

Gelles, D. (2015). *Mindful work: How meditation is changing business from the inside out.* New York, NY: Houghton Mifflin. Contains numerous examples of how mindfulness programs are thriving in companies and shares his personal journey with mindfulness.

Germer, C. K. (2009). *The mindful path to self-compassion: Freeing yourself from destructive thoughts and emotions.* New York, NY: The Guilford Press. Excellent resource for developing self-compassion, and letting go of troublesome thoughts.

Gilbert, P. (2009). *The compassionate mind: A new approach to life's challenges.* Oakland, CA: New Harbinger Publications. Outstanding resource for understanding compassion and using it to navigate life's challenges.

Hanson, R. & Mendius, R. (2009). *Buddha's Brain: The practical neuroscience of happiness, love & wisdom*. Oakland, CA: New Harbinger Publications, Inc. Info on changes in the brain with mindfulness.

Huffington, A. (2014). *Thrive: The third metric to redefining success and creating a life of well-being, wisdom, and wonder*. New York, NY: Harmony Books.

Kornfield, J. (2009). *The wise heart: A guide to the universal teachings of Buddhist psychology*. New York, NY: Bantam Books.

Maturano, J. (2014). *Finding the space to lead: A practical guide to mindful leadership*. New York, NY: Bloomsbury Press.

Neff, K. (2011). *Self-compassion: The proven power of being kind to yourself*. New York, NY: Harper Collins. Teaches all of us how to take better care of ourselves through loving compassion.

O'Hagan, M. (2013, October). To pause and protect. *Mindful Magazine*, 43–51.

Rechtschaffen, D. (2014). *The way of mindful education: Cultivating well-being in teachers and students*. New York NY: W. W. Norton & Co. A comprehensive guide to developing strategies for teaching children and adolescents.

Salzberg, S. (2014). *Real happiness at work: Meditations for accomplishment, achievement, and peace*. New York, NY: Workman Publishing.

Siegel, D. J. (2007). *The mindful brain: Reflection and attunement in the cultivation of well-being*. New York, NY: W. W. Norton & Company.

Smalley S. L. & Winston, D. (2010). *Fully present: The science, art, and practice of mindfulness*. Philadelphia, PA: Perseus Books. Help with mindfulness and learning to live in the present moment.

Tan, C.-M., Goleman, D., & Kabat-Zinn, J. (2012). *Search inside yourself: The unexpected path to achieving success, happiness (and world peace)*. New York, NY: Harper One. Bestseller and info for their corporation's work with mindfulness.

Williams, M. & Penman, D. (2011). *Mindfulness: An eight-week plan for finding peace in a frantic world*. New York, NY: Rodale Press.

Williams, M., Teasdale, J., Segal, Z., & Kabat-Zinn, J. (2007). *The mindful way through depression: Freeing yourself from chronic unhappiness*. New York, NY: The Guilford Press. Includes a CD with shortened meditations. Includes CD with shortened meditations.

Mindfulness Books for Parents

Alderfer, L. & MacLean, K. L. (2011). *Mindful monkey, happy panda*. Somerville, MA: Wisdom Publishers.

Biegel, G. M. (2009). *The stress reduction workbook for teen: Mindfulness skills to help you deal with stress*. Oakland, CA: Instant Help Books.

Greenland, S. K. (2010). *The mindful child: How to help your kid manage stress and become happier, kinder, and more compassionate*. New York, NY: Free Press

Kabat-Zinn, M. & Kabat-Zinn, J. (1998). *Everyday blessings: The inner work of mindful parenting*. New York, NY: Hyperion Press.

MacLean, K. L. (2004). *Peaceful piggy meditation*. Chicago, IL: Albert Whitman & Co.

Roegiers, M. (2010). *Take the time: Mindfulness for kids.* Washington, D.C.: Magination Press.

Shapiro, L., Sprague, R., & McKay, M. (2009). *The relaxation and stress reduction workbook for kids: Help for children to cope with stress, anxiety, and transitions.* Oakland, CA: Instant Help Book.

Shapiro, S. & White, C. (2014). *Mindful discipline: A loving approach to setting limits and raising an emotionally intelligent child.* Oakland, CA: New Harbinger Publications.

Sniel, E., foreword by Kabat-Zinn, J. (2013). *Sitting like a frog: Mindfulness exercises for kids (and their parents).* Boston, MA: Includes a 60-minute audio CD of guided exercises read by Myla Kabat-Zinn.

Hanh, T. N. (2012). *A handful of quiet: Happiness in four pebbles.* Berkley, CA: Plum Blossom Books.

Hanh, T. N., Ngiem, C. C., & Vriezen, W. (2011). *Planting seeds: Practicing mindfulness with children.* Berkeley, CA: Parallax Press.

Lantieri, L. (2014). *Building emotional intelligence: Practices to cultivate inner resilience in children.* Boulder, CO: Sounds True. Contains a CD with mindfulness practices for children and adolescents read by Daniel Goleman, PhD, author of *Emotional Intelligence.*

Willard, C. (2010). *The child's mind: Mindfulness practices to help our children be more focused, calm, and relaxed.* Berkeley, CA: Parallax Press.

Music

Uplifting Vibrations of Tibetan Singing Bowls, Thunder, and Rainforest Sounds: Beautiful, resonant sounds.

Steve Halpern Music

Music for Healing: Mind, Body, and Spirit.
Chakra Suite: Music for Meditation, Healing, and Inner Peace.

Videos for Creating a Mindful Society—Kabat-Zinn and Santorelli

http://mindful.org/the-mindful-society/video-talking-about-creating-a-mindful-society

Books for Stress Reduction

Davis, M., Eshelman, E. R., & McKay, M. (2008). *The relaxation and stress reduction workbook* (6th Ed.) Oakland, CA: New Harbinger Publications. A self-help workbook.

Stahl, B. & Goldstein, E. (2010). *A mindfulness-based stress reduction workbook.* Oakland, CA: New Harbinger Publications. A self-help workbook.

Hatha or Gentle, Stretching Yoga

Yoga for Stress Reduction—DVD by Barbara Benagh—Several options for back, neck, total relaxation. All you need is the DVD and a yoga mat, and the relaxation is there within minutes.

Magazines

Mindful—available at Whole Foods and Barnes and Noble. Full of contemporary examples of mindfulness in professional settings and personal lives. Excellent resource to stay current with recent health benefits and scientific findings.

References

Bach, R. (1977). *Illusions: The adventures of a reluctant Messiah.* New York, NY: Delacorte Press.

Bezold, C. (2006). Preventing causes of disease. In D. P. Rakel & N. Faass (eds.), *Complementary medicine in clinical practice* (pp. 41–48). Sudbury, MA: Jones and Bartlett Publishers.

Birnie, K., Speca, M., & Carlson, L. E. (2010). Exploring self-compassion and empathy in the context of mindfulness-based stress reduction (MBSR). *Stress and Health*, 26, 359–71.

Bolman, L. G. & Deal, T. E. (2008). *Reframing organizations: Artistry, choice, and leadership* (4th Ed.). San Francisco, CA: Jossey-Bass.

Boyatzis, R. & McKee, A. (2005). *Resonant leadership.* Boston, MA: Harvard Business School Press.

Boyce, B. (2011). Creating a mindful society. In B. Boyce (ed.), *The mindfulness revolution: Leading psychologists, scientists, artists, and meditation teachers on the power of mindfulness in daily life* (pp. 252–64). Boston, MA: Shambhala Publications.

Boyce, B. (2012, March). Taking the measure of the mind. *Shambhala Sun*, 43–49; 81–82.

Brown, K. W. & Ryan, R. M. (2003). The benefits of being present: Mindfulness and its role in psychological well-being. *Journal of Personality and Social Psychology*, 84(4), 822–48. doi: 10.1037/0022-351484.4.822.

Brown, K. W., Ryan, R. M., & Creswell, D. (2007). Mindfulness: Theoretical foundations and evidence for its salutary effects. *Psychological Inquiry: An International Journal for the Advancement of Psychological Theory*, 18(4), 211–37.

Bryk, A., Schneider, B. (2004). *Trust in Schools: A Core Resource for Improvement.* New York, NY: Russell Sage.

Carmody, J. & Baer, R. A. (2007). Relationships between mindfulness practice and levels of mindfulness, medical and psychological symptoms and well-being in a mindfulness-based stress reduction program. *Journal of Behavioral Medicine*, 31, 23–33.

Davidson, R. J. & Begley, S. (2012). *The emotional life of your brain.* New York, NY: Hudson Press.

Davidson, R. J., Dunne, J., Eccles, J. S., Engle, A., Greenberg, M., Jennings, P., . . . Vago, D. (2012). Contemplative practices and mental training: Prospects for American education. *Child Development Perspectives,* 6(2), 146–53. doi: 10.1011/j.1750-8606.2012.00240x.

Davidson, R. J. & Kabat-Zinn, J., eds. (2011). *The mind's own physician: A scientific dialogue with the Dalai Lama on the healing power of meditation.* Oakland, CA: New Harbinger Publications, Inc.

Davis, M., Eshelman, E. R., & McKay, M. (2000). *The relaxation and stress reduction workbook,* 5th Ed. Oakland, CA; New Harbinger Publications.

Dillon, K. (2001, April). I think of my failures as a gift. *Harvard Business Review,* 86–89.

Dyrbye, L. N. & Shanafelt, T. D. (2011). Physician burnout: A potential threat to successful health care reform. *Journal of American Medical Association,* 305(19), 2009–10.

Edmondson, A. C. (2011, April). Strategies for learning from failure. *Harvard Business Review,* 48–55.

Epstein, R. M. & Krasner, M. S. (2013). Physician resilience: What it means, why it matters, and how to promote it. *Academic Medicine,* 88(3), 301–3. doi: 10.1097/ACM.0b013e31828cff0.

Fink, D. & Brayman, C. (2006). School leadership succession and the challenges of change. *Educational Administration Quarterly,* 42(1), 62–89. doi: 10.1177/0031316.

Fischer, N. (2011). Mindfulness for everyone. In B. Boyce (ed.), *The mindfulness revolution: Leading psychologists, scientists, artists, and meditation teachers on the power of mindfulness in daily life* (pp. 49–56). Boston, MA: Shambhala.

Flook, L., Goldberg, S. B., Pinger, L., & Davidson, R. J. (2015). Promoting prosocial behavior and self-regulatory skills in preschool children through a mindfulness-based kindness curriculum. *Developmental Psychology,* 51(1), 48–51. doi: org/10.1037/a0038256.

Flook, L., Goldberg, S. B., Pinger, L., Bonus, K., & Davidson, R. J. (2013). Mindfulness for teachers: A pilot study to assess effects on stress, burnout, and teaching efficacy. *Mind, Brain, and Education Society,* 7(3), 182–95.

Fries, M. (2009, July). Mindfulness based stress reduction for the changing work environment. *Journal of Academic and Business Ethics,* 2, 1–10.

Fry, L. & Kriger, M. (2009). Towards a theory of being-centered leadership: Multiple levels of being as context for effective leadership. *Human Relations,* 62(11), 1667–96. doi: 10.1177/0018726709346380.

Fullan, M. (2001). *Leading in a culture of change.* San Francisco, CA: Jossey-Bass.

Gable, M. (2014, October). The doctor is not well. *Mindful Magazine.* 53–57.

Garland, E. L. (2007). The meaning of mindfulness: A second-order cybernetics of stress, metacognition, and coping. *Complementary Health Practice Review,* 12(1), 15–30. doi: 10.1177/153321010731740.

Garland, E. & Gaylord, S. (2009). Envisioning a future contemplative science of mindfulness: Fruitful methods and new content for the next wave of research. *Complementary Health Practice Review*, 14(3), 3–9. doi: 10.1177/1533210109333718.

Gelles, D. (2015). *Mindful work: How meditation is changing business from the inside out.* New York, NY: Houghton Mifflin.

Germer, C. K. (2009). *The mindful path to self-compassion: Freeing yourself from destructive thoughts and emotions.* New York, NY: Guilford Press.

Germer, C. K. & Neff, K. D. (2013). Self-compassion in clinical practice. *Journal of Clinical Psychology: In Session*, 69(8), 856–67. doi: 10.1002/jclp.22021.

Gilbert, P. (2009). *The compassionate mind: A new approach to life's challenges.* Oakland, CA: New Harbinger Publications, Inc.

Gino, F. & Pisano, G. P (2011, April). Why leaders don't learn from success: Failures get a postmortem. Why not triumphs. *Harvard Business Review*. 68–74.

Ginsberg, R. (2008). Being boss is hard: The emotional side of being in charge. *Phi Delta Kappan*, 90(4), 292–97.

Glass, T. E., Bjork, L., & Brunner, C. C. (2000). *The study of the American school superintendency 2000.* Arlington, VA: American Association of School Administrators.

Goleman, D. (2000). *Working with emotional intelligence.* New York, NY: Bantam Books.

Goleman, D. (2006). *Social intelligence: The revolutionary new science of human relationships.* New York, NY: Bantam Books.

Goleman, D. (2013). *Focus: The hidden driver of excellence.* New York, NY: Harper Collins.

Goleman, D. & Boyatzis, R. (2008, September). Social intelligence and the biology of leadership. *Harvard Business Review*, 74–81.

Goleman, D., Boyatzis, R., & McKee, A. (2002). *Primal leadership: Realizing the power of emotional intelligence.* Boston, MA: Harvard Business School Publishing.

Gonzalez, M. (2012). *Mindful leadership: The 9 ways to self-awareness; transforming yourself, and inspiriting others.* San Francisco, CA: Jossey-Bass.

Greenleaf, R. K. (1977). *Servant leadership: A journey into the nature of legitimate power and greatness.* New York, NY: Paulist Press.

Greeson, J. M. (2009). Mindfulness research update: 2008. *Complementary Health Practice Review*, 11, 10–18.

Grubb, W. N., Flessa, J. J. (2006). "A Job Too Big for One": Multiple Principals and Other Nontraditional Approaches to School Leadership. *Educational Administration Quarterly*, 42 (4), 518–55.

Hawk, N. & Martin, B. (2011). Understanding and reducing stress in the superintendency. *Educational Management Administration and Leadership*, 39(3), 364–89. doi: 10.1177/17411432039400.

Heifetz, R. A., Grashow, A., & Linsky, M. (2009). *The practice of adaptive leadership: Tools and tactics for changing your organization and the world.* Boston, MA: Harvard Business Review Press.

Heifetz, R., Grashow, A., & Linsky, M. (2009, July–August). Leadership in a permanent crisis. *Harvard Business Review*, 62–69.

Heifetz, R. A. & Linsky, M. (2002). *Leadership on the line: Staying alive through the dangers of leading.* Boston, MA: Harvard Business Review Press.

Hölzel, B. K, Lazar, S. W., Gard, T., Schuman-Olivier, Z., Vago, D. R., & Ott, U. (2011). How does mindfulness meditation work? Proposing mechanisms of action from a conceptual and neural perspective. *Perspectives on Psychological Science*, 6(6), 537–59. doi: 10.11771745691611419671.

Howley, A., Andrianaivo, S., & Perry, J. (2005). The pain outweighs the gain: Why teachers don't want to become principals. *Teachers College Record*, 107(4), 757–82.

Hunter, J. (2013, April). Is mindfulness good for business? *Mindful Magazine*, 52–59.

Jennings, P. A. (2015). *Mindfulness for teachers: Simple skills for peace and productivity in the classroom*. New York, NY: W. W. Norton & Co.

Johnson, J. (2004). What school leaders want: A public agenda/Wallace foundation survey. *Educational Leadership*, 61(7), 24–27.

Kabat-Zinn, J. (2003). Mindfulness-based interventions in context: Past, present, and future. *Clinical Psychology: Science and Practice*, 10, 144–56.

Kabat-Zinn, J. (2009). *Full catastrophe living: Using the wisdom of your body and mind to face stress, pain, and illness, 15th Anniversary Ed*. New York, NY: Bantam House.

Kabat-Zinn, J. (2012). *Mindfulness for beginners: Reclaiming the present moment and your life*. Boulder, CO: Sounds True.

Kelley, C. & Peterson, K. D. (2007). The work of principals and their preparation: Addressing critical needs for the twenty-first century. In M. Fullan (ed.), *Educational Leadership, 2nd Ed*. (pp. 351–401). San Francisco, CA: Jossey-Bass.

Kotter, J. P. & Cohen, D. S. (2002). *The heart of change: Real-life stories of how people change their organization*. Boston, MA: Harvard Business School Press.

Kouzes, J., Posner, B. (2012). *The Leadership Challenge*. San Francisco, CA: Jossey-Bass.

Krasner, M. S., Epstein, R. M., Beckman, H., Suchman, A. L., Chapman, C. J., Mooney, C. J., & Quill, T. E. (2009). Association of an educational program in mindful communication with burnout, empathy, and attitudes among primary care physicians. *Journal of American Medical Association*, 302(12), 1284–93.

Langer, E. J. (1997). *The power of mindful learning*. Cambridge, MA: Da Capo Press.

Lomatewama, R. *Silent Winds: Poetry Of One Hopi*. Flagstaff, AZ: Badger Claw Press

Louis, K. S., Wahlstom, K. L., Michlin, M., Gordon, M., Thomas, E., Leithwood, K., & Moore, S. (2010). *Learning from leadership: Investigating the links to improved student learning* (Final report to the Wallace Foundation). Minneapolis, MN: The university of Minnesota.

McKee, A., Boyatzis R., & Johnston, F. (2008). *Becoming a resonant leader: Develop your emotional intelligence, renew your relationships, sustain your effectiveness*. Boston, MA: Harvard Business Press.

Maslach, C. & Leiter, M. P. (2008). Early predictors of job burnout and engagement. *Journal of Applied Psychology*, 93, 493–512.

Maturano, J. (2014, February). Taking the space to lead. *Mindful Magazine*, 52–48.

Minter, S. (1991). Relieving workplace stress. *Occupational Hazards*, 53(4), 38–43.

Murphy, J. T. (2011, September). Dancing in the rain: Tips of thriving as a leader in tough times. *Phi Delta Kappan*, 93(1), 36–41.

Neff, K. (2011). *Self-compassion: The proven power of being kind to yourself.* New York: NY: Harper Collins.

Neff, K. D. (2003). The development and validation of a scale to measure self-compassion. *Self and Identity*, 2(3), 223–50. doi: 10.1080/15298860309027.

Neff, K. (2004). Self-compassion and psychological well-being. *Constructivism in the Human Sciences*, 9(2), 27–37.

Neff, K. D., Rude, S., & Kirkpatrick, K. L. (2007). An examination of self-compassion in relation to positive psychological functioning and personality traits. *Journal of Research in Personality*, 41, 908–16.

Northouse, P. G. (2013). *Leadership: Theory and practice* (6th Ed.). Los Angeles, CA: Sage Publications.

Olendzki, A. (2013). The construction of mindfulness. In M. G. Williams and J. Kabat-Zinn (eds.), *Mindfulness: Diverse perspectives on its meaning, origins and application* (pp. 55–70). New York, NY: Routledge.

Overholser, J. C. & Fisher, L. B. (2009). Contemporary perspectives on stress management: Medication, mediation or mitigation. *Journal of Contemporary Psychotherapy*, 39, 147–55. doi: 10. 1007s10879-009-9114-8.

Papa, R., English, F., Davidson, F., Culver, M. K., & Brown, R. (2013). Contours of great leadership: The science, art, and wisdom of outstanding practice. New York, NY: Rowman & Littlefield Education.

Rechtschaffen. D. (2014). *The Way of Mindful Education: Cultivating Well-Being in Teachers and Students.* New York, NY: W.W. Norton & Co.

Reiss, H. (2010, October). Empathy in medicine—a neurobiological perspective. *Journal of American Medical Association*, 304(14), 1604–605.

Rosenzweig, S., Keibel, D. K., Greeson, J. M., Brainard, G. C., & Hojat, M. (2009). Mindfulness-based stress reduction lowers psychological stress in medical students. *Teaching and Learning in Medicine: An International Journal*, 15(2), 88–92.

Ryback, D. (2006). Self-determination and the neurology of mindfulness. *Journal of Humanistic Psychology*, 46(4), 474–93.

Seyfarth, J. T. (2007). *Human Resources Management for Effective Schools.* New York, NY: Pearson.

Shanafelt, T. D., Sloan, J. A., & Habermann, T. M. (2003). The well-being of physicians. *American Journal of Medicine*, 1146(6), 513–19.

Shapiro, S. L. & Carlson, L. E. (2009). *The art and science of mindfulness: Integrating mindfulness into psychology and the helping professions.* Washington, D.C.: American Psychological Association.

Shapiro, S. L., Carlson, L. E., Astin, J. A., & Freedman, B. (2006). Mechanisms of mindfulness. *Journal of Clinical Psychology*, 62(3), 373–88. doi: 10.1002/jclp.20237.

Shapiro, S. L., Oman, D., Thoresen, C. E., Plante, T. G., & Flinders, T. (2008). Cultivating mindfulness: Effects on well-being. *Journal of Clinical Psychology*, 64(7), 840–62. doi: 10.1002/jclp.20491.

Smalley, S. & Winston, D. (2010). *Fully present: The science, art, and practice of mindfulness.* Philadelphia, PA: DeCapo Lifelong Books.

Smalley, S. & Winston, D. (2011). Is mindfulness for you? In B. Boyce (ed.), *The mindfulness revolution: Leading psychologists, scientists, artists, and meditation teachers on the power of mindfulness in daily life* (pp. 11–20). Boston, MA: Shambhala.

Sorenson, R. D. (2007). Stress management in education: Warning signs and coping mechanisms, *Management in Education*, 21(3), 10–13.

Sytsma, S. (2009). The educational leader's alchemy: Creating the gold within. *Management in Education*, 23, 78–84.

Stahl, B. & Goldstein, E. (2010). *A mindfulness-based stress reduction workbook.* Oakland, CA: New Harbinger Publications, Inc.

Stanton, J. M., Balzar, W. K., Smith, P. C., Parra, L. F., & Ironson, G. (2001) A general measure of work stress: The stress in general scale. *Educational and Psychological Measurement*, 61, 866–88.

Tan, C.-M. (2012). *Search inside yourself: The unexpected path to achieving success, happiness (and world peace).* New York, NY: Harper One.

Teasdale, J. D., Segal, Z. V., & Williams, J. M. (2003). Mindfulness training and problem formulation. *Clinical Psychology: Science and practice*, 10(2), 157–60. doi: 10.1093/clipsy/bpg017.

Weinzimmer, L. G. & McConoughey, J. (2013). *The wisdom of failure: How to learn the tough leadership lessons without paying the price.* San Francisco, CA: Jossey-Bass.

Weinzimmer, L. G. & McConoughey, J. (2013). *The wisdom of failure: How to learn the tough leadership lessons without paying the price.* San Francisco, CA: Jossey-Bass.

Wells, C. M. (2015). Conceptualizing mindful leadership: How the practice of mindfulness informs the practice of leading. *Educational Leadership Review Doctoral Research*, 2(1), 1–23.

Wells, C. M. (2013a). Mindfulness in academia: Considerations for administrative preparation. *Education Leadership Review*, 14(3), 1–12.

Wells, C. M. (2013b). Educational leaders describe a job too big for one: Stress reduction in the midst of leading. *AASA Journal of Scholarship and Practice*, 10(2), 32–45.

Wells, C. M. (2013c). Principals responding to constant pressure: Finding a source of stress management. *NASSP The Bulletin, XX*(X), 1–15. doi: 10.1177/0192636513504453.

Wells, C. M., Maxfield, C. R., & Klocko, B. A. (2011). Complexities inherent in the workloads of principals: Implications for teacher leadership. In B. J. Alford, G. Perrerault, L. Zellner, & J. W. Ballenger (eds.), *2011 NCPEA Yearbook: Blazing Trails: Preparing Leaders to Improve Access and Equity in Today's Schools* (pp. 29–46). Lancaster, PA: DEStech Publications, Inc., Pro>Active Publications.

Williams, M. & Penman, D. (2011). *Mindfulness: An eight-week plan for finding peace in a frantic world.* New York, NY: Rodale.

Winter, P. A., Rinehart, J. S., Keely, J. L., & Bjork, L. G. (2007). Superintendent recruitment: A statewide assessment of principal attraction to the job. *Planning and Changing*, 38(1&2), 35–59.

Index

About the Author

Caryn M. Wells, PhD, is associate professor in educational and teacher leadership in the Department of Organizational Leadership at Oakland University in Rochester, Michigan. She teaches mindfulness for educational leaders in her graduate classes, and presents the introduction to mindfulness to doctoral and medical students at the university. Dr. Wells consults with professional organizations and presents trainings for teachers and school leaders in mindfulness, stress reduction, and mindful leadership. She is a former teacher of English, counselor, and assistant principal and principal, all at the high-school level.